The Sain...

SOUPS & STARTERS
Caroline Ellwood

CONTENTS

NOTES

Standard spoon measurements are used in all recipes
1 tablespoon = one 15 ml spoon
1 teaspoon = one 5 ml spoon
All spoon measures are level.

Fresh herbs are used unless otherwise stated. If unobtainable substitute a bouquet garni of the equivalent dried herbs, or use dried herbs instead but halve the quantities stated.

Use freshly ground black pepper where pepper is specified.

Ovens should be preheated to the specified temperature.

For all recipes, quantities are given in both metric and imperial measures. Follow either set but not a mixture of both, because they are not interchangeable.

Recipes for basic stocks to use in soups, plus ideas for garnishes are given on pages 6-7.

Published exclusively for
J Sainsbury plc
Stamford Street, London SE1 9LL
by Cathay Books
59 Grosvenor Street, London W1

First published 1982
Reprinted 1983, 1984

© Cathay Books 1982
ISBN 0 86178 162 7

Printed in Hong Kong

INTRODUCTION

Most meals are off to a good start if you begin with a super soup or starter. Delicious homemade soups are not only perfect as inexpensive starters but are just as good served with crisp French bread for a supper snack or lunch dish.

Most soups are quick and easy to prepare and can be made in advance and frozen – a real help for the cook. The all-important basis of a good soup is the stock. It really is worth taking the time to prepare a rich flavoured homemade stock but if you are in a hurry, a good standby is canned consommé which is an excellent substitute. Commercially made stock cubes can be used but the result is not as good and soups made this way tend to have a similar taste. A blender or food processor is invaluable for soup-making, especially if you want a smooth and velvety texture.

The first course should contrast with the rest of the meal and be a mouth-watering appetizer for the dishes to follow. Whether the starter is hot or cold, sweet or savoury, serve small portions just to stimulate the appetite.

Enjoy trying these recipes and *bon appétit!*

Beef Stock

500 g (1 lb) marrow
    bone, or knuckle
    of veal, chopped
500 g (1 lb) shin of
    beef, chopped
2 large onions
3 carrots
2 sticks celery
1 clove garlic, sliced
1 bouquet garni
salt and pepper
150 ml (¼ pint) dry
    red wine
    (optional)

Put the marrow bone and beef in a roasting pan. Cook for about 1 hour in a preheated moderate oven, 180°C (350°F), Gas Mark 4, until browned.

Put the bones and meat in a large pan. Chop the vegetables and add to the pan with the garlic, bouquet garni and salt and pepper to taste. Pour over the wine, if using, and sufficient water to cover. Bring to the boil and remove any scum. Cover and simmer for 3 hours.

Remove any fat from the surface with kitchen paper, then strain.

Store in the refrigerator for up to 2 days and use as required.
Makes about 1.5 litres (2½ pints)

Chicken Stock

1 chicken carcass plus
    giblets
1 chicken portion
2 large onions
4 carrots
1 leek
3 sticks celery
1 bouquet garni
salt and pepper
cold water to cover
2 tablespoons dry
    sherry

Put the chicken carcass, giblets and portion in a large pan. Chop the vegetables and add to the pan with the bouquet garni and salt and pepper to taste. Pour in sufficient water to cover and bring to the boil. Remove any scum. Cover and simmer for 3 to 3½ hours.

Strain and remove any fat from the surface. Stir in the sherry.

Store in the refrigerator for up to 2 days and use as required.
Makes about 1.5 litres (2½ pints)

Fish Stock

1 large onion,
    chopped
2 leeks, chopped
375 g (12 oz) fish
    bones and heads
salt and pepper
1 bouquet garni
water to cover
150 ml (¼ pint) dry
    white wine

Put the onion and leeks into a large pan with the fish bones and heads. Season well with salt and pepper and add the bouquet garni. Cover with cold water, bring to the boil and skim. Cover and simmer for 1 hour.

Strain. Stir in the wine and store in the refrigerator for up to 1 day. Use as required.
Makes about 750 ml (1¼ pints)

GARNISHES

Any soup or starter can be transformed into something special by adding an attractive garnish. A simple but effective soup garnish is a swirl of cream sprinkled with freshly chopped herbs, like chives or parsley.

Croûtons complement most soups. To make them, simply cut bread into 5 mm – 1 cm (¼ – ½ inch) cubes, or use small pastry cutters to make fancy shapes like stars, hearts, etc., then fry the croûtons in a little butter until crisp and golden all over. Garlic croûtons can be made by adding a crushed clove of garlic to the butter before frying.

Other simple ideas for soups include: toasted flaked almonds; small bacon rolls; saffron rice; crumbled bacon.

A julienne of vegetables makes an unusual soup garnish: Cook strips of carrot, celery or leek in boiling salted water until soft. Another idea is fried parsley: fry small sprigs of parsley in hot oil for a few moments; drain well.

Many garnishes are ideal for both soups and starters: sprigs of fresh herbs; lemon or lime slices or wedges; cucumber slices, onion rings and olives.

HOT SOUPS

Wine Consommé

1 large onion,
    roughly chopped
2 celery sticks,
    roughly chopped
4 carrots, roughly
    chopped
1 bouquet garni
2 × 411 g (14½ oz)
    cans beef consommé
250 ml (8 fl oz) dry
    red wine
julienne of vegetables
    to garnish

Put the onion, celery, carrots and bouquet garni in a pan. Add the consommé, bring slowly to the boil, cover and simmer for 30 minutes.

Cool slightly, then strain and return to the pan. Add the wine, bring to the boil and simmer, uncovered, for 2 minutes.

Serve garnished with a julienne of vegetables.

Serves 6

Mushroom Soup with Madeira

75 g (3 oz) butter
1 large onion, finely
   chopped
500 g (1 lb)
   mushrooms, finely
   chopped
25 g (1 oz) plain
   flour
900 ml (1½ pints)
   chicken stock
salt and pepper
120 ml (4 fl oz) dry
   madeira
150 ml (¼ pint)
   double cream
chopped parsley to
   garnish

Melt the butter in a large pan, add the onion and cook for 20 minutes or until evenly browned. Add the mushrooms and cook for 2 minutes.

Stir in the flour and cook for 1 minute. Gradually stir in the stock, then season with salt and pepper to taste. Bring to the boil, cover and simmer for 10 minutes.

Stir in the madeira and cream and heat through gently. Serve immediately, garnished with parsley.

Serves 4 to 6

Fennel Soup

25 g (1 oz) butter
1 onion, chopped
4 bulbs fennel,
  chopped
1 bouquet garni
900 ml (1½ pints)
  chicken stock
salt and pepper
3 egg yolks
juice of 1 lemon
TO GARNISH:
fennel leaves
croûtons

Melt the butter in a large pan, add the onion and fry for 5 minutes, without browning. Stir in the fennel, then add the bouquet garni, stock and salt and pepper to taste. Bring to the boil, cover and simmer for 30 minutes, until the vegetables are very tender.

Remove the bouquet garni and cool slightly. Sieve or work in an electric blender until smooth, then reheat. Mix the egg yolks and lemon juice together with a few tablespoons of the soup.

Stir the egg mixture into the soup and serve immediately, garnished with fennel leaves and croûtons.
Serves 6

Cream of Chicken Soup

1 large onion,
  chopped
2 celery sticks,
  chopped
2 large carrots,
  chopped
1 leek, chopped
1 × 1.25 kg
  (2½ lb) chicken
1 bouquet garni
1 blade mace
grated rind and juice
  of ½ lemon
salt
40 g (1½ oz) butter
40 g (1½ oz) plain
  flour
2 egg yolks
150 ml (¼ pint)
  double cream

Put the vegetables and chicken in a large pan and pour over enough water to cover. Add the bouquet garni, mace, lemon rind and juice, and salt to taste. Bring slowly to the boil, skim, then cover and simmer for 1 hour, until the chicken is tender.

Take out the chicken and cut off about 250 g (8 oz) meat. Dice and set aside. Strain the stock and reserve 1.2 litres (2 pints). Leave to cool, then skim off any fat.

Melt the butter in a pan, stir in the flour and cook for 1 minute, without browning. Gradually stir in the reserved stock. Bring to the boil. Simmer for 2 minutes, then add the diced chicken and heat through.

Blend the egg yolks and cream together. Remove the soup from the heat and stir in the cream mixture. Serve immediately.
Serves 6
NOTE: Use the rest of the chicken for another dish.

Artichoke and Parsley Soup

1 kg (2 lb) Jerusalem
  artichokes
juice of 1 lemon
25 g (1 oz) butter
1 large onion,
  chopped
600 ml (1 pint)
  chicken stock
300 ml (½ pint)
  milk
salt
150 ml (¼ pint)
  single cream
2 tablespoons finely
  chopped parsley

Peel and chop the artichokes. Place in
a bowl with the lemon juice and
enough water to cover.

Melt the butter in a large pan, add
the onion and cook until transparent
but not coloured. Drain the
artichokes and add to the pan with
the stock, milk, and salt to taste.
Bring to the boil, cover and simmer
for 35 to 40 minutes, until the
vegetables are tender. Cool slightly.

Sieve or work in an electric
blender until smooth. Return to the
pan and reheat. Stir in the cream and
parsley and serve immediately.
Serves 4 to 6

11

Tomato and Cheese Soup

25 g (1 oz) butter
2 large onions,
   chopped
25 g (1 oz) plain
   flour
1 kg (2 lb) tomatoes,
   skinned, seeded
   and chopped
1 clove garlic,
   crushed
1 rosemary sprig
1 thyme sprig
600 ml (1 pint)
   chicken stock
salt and pepper
150 ml (¼ pint)
   double cream
1 egg yolk
125 g (4 oz)
   Gruyère cheese,
   grated

Melt the butter in a pan, add the onions and cook, without browning, for 10 minutes. Stir in the flour and cook for a further minute. Stir in the tomatoes, garlic, herbs, stock, and salt and pepper to taste.

Bring to the boil, cover and simmer for 30 minutes or until the tomatoes are very tender. Cool slightly, then sieve or work in an electric blender until smooth. Return to the pan.

Blend the cream and egg yolk together and stir into the pan. Heat through gently; do not boil or the soup will curdle.

Stir in the cheese and serve immediately.
Serves 6 to 8

Cream of Cheddar Soup

40 g (1½ oz) butter
3 large onions, finely
   chopped
2 × 411 g (14½ oz)
   cans beef or
   chicken consommé
120 ml (4 fl oz) dry
   white wine
1 bouquet garni
salt and pepper
8 slices French bread,
   1 cm (½ inch)
   thick, toasted
8 slices Gruyère
   cheese, 5 mm
   (¼ inch) thick
3 tablespoons grated
   Parmesan cheese
50 g (2 oz) Cheddar
   cheese, grated

Melt the butter in a pan, add the onions and cook until golden brown; this will take about 30 minutes. Add the consommé, wine, bouquet garni, and salt and pepper to taste. Bring to the boil, cover and simmer for 20 minutes. Remove the bouquet garni.

Arrange a layer of toast in the bottom of an ovenproof tureen or deep casserole. Cover with a layer of Gruyère, then sprinkle with Parmesan and Cheddar. Repeat these layers once or twice more, finishing with a layer of cheese.

Pour over the onion–flavoured stock and place in a preheated moderate oven, 180°C (350°F), Gas Mark 4, for 20 minutes, until the cheese has melted.

Serve immediately.

Serves 4 to 6

NOTE: This is a delicious, substantial soup. It makes a good main course, served with a crisp salad.

Cream of Chestnut Soup

500 g (1 lb)
  chestnuts
1 tablespoon oil
125 g (4 oz) back
  bacon, derinded
  and diced
1 large onion,
  chopped
2 celery sticks,
  chopped
2 carrots, chopped
1 bouquet garni
1.2 litres (2 pints)
  chicken stock
salt and white pepper
TO GARNISH:
fried bacon rolls
fried chopped parsley

Put the chestnuts in a pan of cold water, bring to the boil and simmer for 1 minute. Remove from the pan with a slotted spoon.

Hold each chestnut in a cloth and peel away the outer and inner skins with a sharp knife. If the skin does not come away, return to the pan for 1 minute.

Heat the oil in a large pan, add the bacon and onion and fry for 2 minutes, without browning. Add the celery, carrots and bouquet garni. Stir in the stock and season with salt and pepper to taste. Add the skinned whole chestnuts and bring to the boil. Cover and simmer for 1 hour, until the chestnuts are soft. Discard the bouquet garni and cool slightly.

Sieve or work in an electric blender until smooth. Return to the pan and reheat.

Garnish with bacon rolls and parsley to serve.
Serves 8

Cream of Sweetcorn Soup

40 g (1½ oz) butter
1 onion, chopped
2 potatoes, diced
25 g (1 oz) plain
  flour
900 ml (1½ pints)
  milk
1 bay leaf
salt and white pepper
2 × 326 g (11½ oz)
  cans sweetcorn,
  drained
2 tablespoons double
  cream
crumbled fried bacon,
  to garnish

Melt the butter in a pan, add the onion and cook for 5 minutes, without browning. Add the potatoes and cook for a further 2 minutes.

Stir in the flour, then gradually add the milk, stirring constantly. Bring to the boil, add the bay leaf and salt and pepper to taste. Add half of the sweetcorn, cover and simmer for 15 to 20 minutes. Discard the bay leaf and cool slightly.

Sieve or work in an electric blender until smooth. Return to the pan, add the remaining sweetcorn and heat through.

Stir in the cream, sprinkle over the bacon and serve immediately.
Serves 4 to 6

Garlic Soup

2 tablespoons olive
    oil
24 cloves garlic,
    peeled
900 ml (1½ pints)
    beef or chicken
    stock
1 bouquet garni
pinch of grated
    nutmeg
1 blade mace
salt and pepper
3 egg yolks
6-8 slices bread
TO FINISH:
chopped parsley
grated Parmesan
    cheese

Heat the oil in a large pan, add the
whole garlic cloves and fry, without
browning, for 10 minutes.

Stir in the stock and add the
bouquet garni, nutmeg, mace, and
salt and pepper to taste. Bring to the
boil, cover and simmer for
20 minutes.

Blend the egg yolks with 2 tablespoons of the soup. Strain the
remaining soup and return to the
pan. Bring to the boil, then remove
from the heat. Set aside for
2 minutes.

Meanwhile, toast the bread on
both sides and place in individual
soup bowls.

Pour the egg yolk mixture into the
soup, stirring constantly. Ladle into
the bowls and serve at once,
garnished with chopped parsley.
Hand the Parmesan cheese separately.
Serves 6 to 8

Sweet Pepper Soup

40 g (1½ oz) butter
1 large onion, finely
    chopped
1 clove garlic, crushed
25 g (1 oz) plain
    flour
900 ml (1½ pints)
    chicken stock
500 g (1 lb) red
    peppers, cored,
    seeded and chopped
1 dried red chilli,
    chopped
250 g (8 oz)
    tomatoes, skinned,
    seeded and chopped
1 teaspoon chopped
    thyme
chopped chives to
    garnish

Melt the butter in a large pan, add
the onion and garlic and fry gently
for 2 minutes. Stir in the flour and
cook for a further 2 minutes.
Gradually add the stock, stirring
constantly, and bring to the boil.

Add the red peppers, chilli,
tomatoes and thyme. Cover and
simmer for 20 to 25 minutes, until
the vegetables are tender. Cool
slightly.

Sieve or work in an electric
blender until smooth. Return to the
pan and heat through. Garnish with
chives before serving.
Serves 6

Aubergine and Crab Soup

1 tablespoon oil
2 large onions,
   chopped
2 cloves garlic, crushed
4 large aubergines,
   peeled and
   chopped
1 × 397 g (14 oz)
   can tomatoes
300 ml (½ pint)
   chicken stock
1 tablespoon tomato
   purée
1 bouquet garni
120 ml (4 fl oz) dry
   white wine
salt and pepper
1 × 177 g (6 oz)
   can crabmeat,
   drained and flaked
chopped parsley to
   garnish

Heat the oil in a pan, add the onions and garlic and cook for 5 to 7 minutes, without browning. Stir in the aubergines and the tomatoes with their juice. Bring slowly to the boil and stir in the stock, tomato purée, bouquet garni and wine. Season with salt and pepper to taste. Cover and simmer for 30 minutes, until the vegetables are very tender. Discard the bouquet garni and cool slightly.

Sieve or work in an electric blender until smooth. Return to the pan, stir in the crabmeat and bring to the boil.

Serve immediately, garnished with chopped parsley.
Serves 6

Seafood Saffron Soup

2 large onions,
  chopped
250 g (8 oz)
  potatoes, diced
600 ml (1 pint) milk
300 ml (½ pint) fish
  or chicken stock
750 g (1½ lb) white
  fish fillets
4 shelled scallops,
  roughly chopped
120 ml (4 fl oz)
  white wine
1 teaspoon powdered
  saffron
salt and pepper
125 g (4 oz) peeled
  prawns
150 ml (¼ pint)
  double cream
few unshelled cooked
  prawns to garnish

Put the onions and potatoes in a pan,
add the milk and stock and bring to
the boil. Cook for 15 minutes, until
soft. Cool slightly, then sieve or
work in an electric blender until
smooth.

Cut the fish into 4 cm (1½ inch)
pieces. Return the soup to the pan
and add the fish and scallops. Cook
gently for about 10 minutes, until
tender. Stir in the wine and saffron,
and season with salt and pepper to
taste.

Stir in the prawns and cream and
serve immediately, garnished with
prawns.
Serves 4 to 6

Mussel Chowder

1 kg (2 lb) mussels
  in shells
250 g (8 oz) white
  fish fillets, skinned
40 g (1½ oz) butter
1 onion, chopped
2 celery sticks, chopped
1 clove garlic, crushed
25 g (1 oz) plain
  flour
900 ml (1½ pints)
  fish stock
150 ml (¼ pint) dry
  white wine
salt and white pepper
1 bouquet garni
50 g (2 oz) long-
  grain rice, cooked
2 strands saffron
2 egg yolks
3 tablespoons cream
2 tablespoons
  chopped parsley

Scrub the mussels clean and cut the
fish into 4 cm (1½ inch) pieces.

Melt the butter in a pan, add the
onion, celery and garlic and cook for
2 minutes, without browning. Stir in
the flour and cook for 2 minutes.
Gradually stir in the stock and bring
to the boil. Stir in the wine, and
season with salt and pepper to taste.

Add the fish, bouquet garni and
mussels. Cover and cook for 5 to
7 minutes or until the fish is tender
and the mussel shells have opened;
discard any that do not. Stir in the
rice and saffron, and heat through.
Discard the bouquet garni.

Blend the egg yolks and cream
together. Pour 1 tablespoon hot soup
onto the egg mixture and mix well.

Remove the soup from the heat
and stir in the blended mixture with
the parsley. Serve immediately.

Serves 6

Lentil Soup

125 g (4 oz) lentils
25 g (1 oz) butter
2 large onions,
    chopped
4 leeks, chopped
4 carrots, chopped
2 celery sticks,
    chopped
1.2 litres (2 pints)
    beef stock
120 ml (4 fl oz) dry
    sherry
salt and pepper
50 g (2 oz) cooked
    ham, diced
2 tablespoons
    chopped parsley

Soak the lentils in cold water
overnight; rinse and drain.

Melt the butter in a pan, add the
onions and cook until lightly
browned. Stir in the leeks, carrots
and celery and cook for 2 minutes.

Add the lentils to the pan with the
stock, sherry, and salt and pepper to
taste. Bring to the boil, cover and
simmer for 1 hour, or until the
vegetables and lentils are tender.
Cool slightly.

Sieve or work in an electric
blender until smooth. Return to the
pan and heat through. Stir in the
ham and parsley to serve.

Serves 6

Scotch Broth

This soup is substantial enough to be served as a meal.

750 g (1½ lb) neck
  of lamb
900 ml (1½ pints)
  beef stock
1 bouquet garni
salt and pepper
50 g (2 oz) pearl
  barley
250 g (8 oz) carrots,
  sliced
4 celery sticks,
  chopped
2 onions, sliced
2 leeks, sliced
1 turnip, diced
1 small swede, diced
120 ml (4 fl oz) dry
  sherry

Chop the lamb if necessary and
discard any fat. Put in a large pan
with the stock, bouquet garni, and
salt and pepper to taste.

Bring to the boil and remove any
scum. Cover and simmer for
1½ hours, skimming occasionally.

Take out the meat and add the
pearl barley and vegetables to the
pan. Bring to the boil, cover and
simmer for 30 minutes. Discard the
bouquet garni.

Chop the meat from the bone, and
add to the pan with the sherry. Bring
to the boil and simmer for 5 minutes.

Remove any fat from the surface
with kitchen paper before serving.
Serves 6 to 8
NOTE: For best results, make the soup
the day before required. Leave in the
refrigerator overnight. Remove the
solid fat from the surface, then bring
the soup to the boil and heat through.

Mulligatawny Soup

250 g (8 oz) lentils
2 tablespoons oil
2 large onions,
  chopped
1 tablespoon curry
  powder
2 cloves garlic, crushed
1 red pepper, cored,
  seeded and chopped
3 dried chillies,
  chopped
1.2 litres (2 pints)
  chicken stock
25 g (1 oz) seedless
  raisins
250 g (8 oz)
  tomatoes, skinned,
  seeded and chopped
1 tablespoon tomato
  purée
salt and pepper
saffron rice to garnish
  (optional)

Soak the lentils in cold water overnight; rinse and drain.

Heat the oil in a pan, add the onions and fry until browned.

Stir in the curry powder and cook for 2 minutes, stirring occasionally. Add the garlic, lentils and remaining ingredients, with salt and pepper to taste. Bring to the boil, cover and simmer for 1½ hours. Cool slightly.

Sieve or work in an electric blender until smooth. Return to the pan and heat through.

Serve hot, garnished with saffron rice if liked.

Serves 8

NOTE: To make saffron rice, cook rice in boiling salted water with a few saffron strands added, until tender.

Breton-Style Onion Soup

40 g (1½ oz) butter
500 g (1 lb) strong
  onions, sliced
250 g (8 oz)
  potatoes, diced
1.2 litres (2 pints)
  beef stock
1 bouquet garni
salt and pepper
oil for shallow frying
4 cloves garlic, sliced
1 small French loaf,
  sliced into 1 cm
  (½ inch) rounds
50 g (2 oz) Cheddar
  cheese, grated

Melt the butter in a pan, add the onions and cook gently for 30 minutes or until golden brown.

Add the potatoes, stock, bouquet garni, and salt and pepper to taste. Bring to the boil, cover and simmer for 15 to 20 minutes, until the potatoes are tender. Remove the bouquet garni.

Heat the oil in a frying pan with the garlic, then add the French bread and fry until golden brown on both sides; drain.

Ladle the soup into individual heatproof bowls. Float 1 or 2 pieces of bread in each bowl and sprinkle with the cheese. Place under a preheated hot grill until the cheese is bubbling. Serve immediately.

Serves 6 to 8

Curried Parsnip Soup

50 g (2 oz) butter
1 teaspoon curry
   powder
2 large onions,
   chopped
750 g (1½ lb)
   parsnips, chopped
600 ml (1 pint)
   chicken stock
salt and white pepper
300 ml (½ pint)
   milk
150 ml (¼ pint)
   single cream
1 red apple, diced and
   tossed in lemon
   juice, to garnish

Melt the butter in a large pan, stir in the curry powder and cook for 2 minutes. Add the onions and parsnips and cook gently for 5 minutes, stirring occasionally. Add the stock, and salt and pepper to taste.

Bring to the boil and cook for 25 to 30 minutes, until the vegetables are tender. Cool slightly.

Sieve or work in an electric blender until smooth. Return to the pan and add the milk and cream. Bring to the boil, stirring; check the seasoning and serve immediately, garnished with the apple.
Serves 6 to 8

Broad Bean Soup

25 g (1 oz) butter
1 onion, chopped
1 celery stick,
  chopped
25 g (1 oz) plain
  flour
900 ml (1½ pints)
  chicken stock
1.5 kg (3-3½ lb)
  broad beans in
  pods, or 500 g
  (1 lb) shelled
  weight
1 bouquet garni
salt and pepper
2 egg yolks
TO GARNISH:
4-6 tablespoons
  whipped cream
chopped chives

Melt the butter in a large pan, add the onion and celery and cook for 5 minutes, without browning. Stir in the flour and cook for 1 minute.

Gradually stir in the stock, then add the beans, bouquet garni, and salt and pepper to taste. Bring to the boil and simmer for 35 minutes or until the beans are very tender. Remove the bouquet garni and cool slightly. Sieve or work in an electric blender until smooth. Return to the pan.

Blend the egg yolks with 2 to 3 tablespoons of the soup. Reheat the remaining soup, then remove from the heat and leave for 2 minutes. Stir in the egg mixture until smooth.

Pour into individual warmed soup bowls. Top each with cream and chopped chives. Serve immediately.
Serves 4 to 6

Potage Vert

2 bunches of
    watercress
1 bunch of spring
    onions, chopped
250 g (8 oz) spinach
1 rosemary sprig
1 thyme sprig
4 tablespoons
    chopped parsley
600 ml (1 pint)
    chicken stock
salt and pepper
1½ teaspoons
    cornflour
120 ml (4 fl oz)
    double cream
squeeze of lemon
    juice
lemon slices to
    garnish

Put the watercress, spring onions and spinach in a large pan. Add the herbs and pour over the stock. Season with salt and pepper to taste. Bring to the boil, cover and simmer for 20 minutes. Cool slightly.

Sieve or work in an electric blender until smooth. Return to the pan and heat through.

Blend the cornflour with the cream, stir into the soup and bring to simmering point. Cook gently, stirring constantly, until thickened. Stir in the lemon juice.

Serve immediately, garnished with lemon slices.

Serves 4 to 6

Bean Soup

125 g (4 oz) haricot
   beans
50 g (2 oz) each red
   kidney beans and
   dried peas
2 large onions
2 celery sticks
2 large carrots
25 g (1 oz) butter
2 cloves garlic, crushed
1 × 397 g (14 oz)
   can tomatoes
120 ml (4 fl oz) dry
   red wine
300 ml (½ pint) stock
1 bouquet garni
salt and pepper
125 g (4 oz)
   courgettes, sliced
1 tablespoon Worces-
   tershire sauce
1 tablespoon tomato
   purée
PISTOU:
4 cloves garlic
1 bunch basil
4 tablespoons olive oil
25 g (1 oz) pine nuts

Soak all the pulses separately in cold water overnight. Rinse in cold water and drain. Put in a large pan, cover with cold water and bring to the boil; do not add salt at this stage. Boil steadily for 10 minutes, then cover and simmer for 1¼ hours or until the beans are tender; drain.

Chop the onions, celery and carrots. Melt the butter in a large pan, add the onions and fry until golden. Add the garlic, celery and carrots, tomatoes with their juice, the wine, stock, bouquet garni and salt and pepper to taste. Bring to the boil, cover and simmer for 20 minutes, then stir in the courgettes, Worcestershire sauce and tomato purée. Continue cooking for 5 minutes, then add the cooked beans and peas; heat through.

Meanwhile, make the pistou. Pound the garlic with the basil, oil and nuts to a smooth paste. Mix into the soup just before serving.

Serve with grated Cheddar cheese and crusty rolls.
Serves 6 to 8

Courgette Soup

25 g (1 oz) butter
2 large onions,
   chopped
750 g (1½ lb)
   courgettes,
   chopped
2 × 411 g (14½ oz)
   cans consommé
2 tablespoons dry
   sherry
1 bouquet garni
salt and pepper
150 ml (¼ pint)
   double cream
croûtons to garnish

Melt the butter in a pan, add the onions and cook gently for 5 minutes. Stir in the courgettes and cook gently for 10 minutes.

Stir in the consommé and sherry and bring to the boil. Add the bouquet garni and seasoning, cover and simmer for 30 minutes.

Remove the bouquet garni and cool slightly. Sieve or work in an electric blender until smooth. Return to the pan and heat through.

Stir in the cream and serve, garnished with croûtons.
Serves 6

COLD SOUPS

Carrot and Orange Soup

25 g (1 oz) butter
500 g (1 lb) carrots,
   sliced
1 onion, chopped
900 ml (1½ pints)
   chicken stock
pinch of sugar
salt and pepper
grated rind of
   1 orange
juice of 4 oranges
150 ml (¼ pint)
   single cream

Melt the butter in a pan, add the carrots and onion and cook for 10 minutes, without browning.

Add the stock, sugar, and salt and pepper to taste. Bring to the boil, cover and simmer for 1 hour or until the carrots are tender. Cool slightly.

Sieve or work in an electric blender until smooth. Pour into a soup tureen and stir in the orange rind and juice. Leave to cool, then chill for several hours.

Just before serving, stir in the cream.
Serves 6

Vichyssoise

50 g (2 oz) butter
2 large onions,
    chopped
4 large leeks, white
    part only
4 large potatoes,
    diced
1.2 litres (2 pints)
    chicken stock
1 bouquet garni
salt and white pepper
150 ml (¼ pint)
    double cream
TO GARNISH:
2 tablespoons
    chopped chives
croûtons

Melt the butter in a pan, add the onions and cook, without browning, for 10 minutes.

Add the leeks and potatoes and toss well. Stir in the stock and add the bouquet garni, and salt and pepper to taste. Bring to the boil, cover and simmer for 30 to 40 minutes, stirring occasionally. Remove the bouquet garni and cool slightly.

Sieve or work in an electric blender until smooth. Pour into a soup tureen and leave until cool. Stir in the cream. Chill for 3 to 4 hours.

Garnish with chopped chives and croûtons before serving.

Serves 6

Chilled Cucumber and Mint Soup

1 tablespoon oil
1 large onion, finely chopped
2 cucumbers, peeled and diced
1 medium potato, finely chopped
900 ml (1½ pints) chicken stock
1 bouquet garni
salt
150 ml (¼ pint) single cream
2 tablespoons finely chopped mint
mint sprigs to garnish

Heat the oil in a pan, add the onion and cook until transparent. Stir in the cucumber and potato, then add the stock, bouquet garni, and salt to taste. Bring to the boil, cover and simmer for 20 to 25 minutes. Remove the bouquet garni and cool slightly.

Sieve or work in an electric blender until smooth. Pour into a bowl, stir in the cream and mint and chill for 2 to 3 hours before serving.

Serve garnished with mint sprigs.
Serves 4 to 6

Iced Tomato and Basil Soup

1 tablespoon oil
1 large onion, chopped
1 clove garlic, crushed
25 g (1 oz) plain
   flour
1 kg (2 lb) ripe
   tomatoes
1 tablespoon Worces-
   tershire sauce
2 drops Tabasco
   sauce
250 ml (8 fl oz) dry
   white wine
1 tablespoon tomato
   purée
salt and pepper
3 tablespoons
   chopped basil
TO GARNISH:
6 tablespoons double
   cream, whipped
chopped chives

Heat the oil in a large pan, add the onion and garlic and cook for 5 minutes, without browning. Stir in the flour and cook, stirring, for 2 minutes.

Chop the tomatoes roughly and add to the pan. Cover and cook gently for 20 minutes, stirring occasionally.

Add the Worcestershire and Tabasco sauces, wine, tomato purée, and salt and pepper to taste. Bring to the boil, cover and simmer for 30 minutes. Cool slightly.

Sieve or work in an electric blender until smooth then strain into a bowl.

Leave to cool, then stir in the basil and chill for several hours.

Pour into individual soup bowls. Top each with a swirl of cream and chopped chives. Serve immediately.
Serves 6

Iced Avocado Soup

2 ripe avocados
juice of ½ lemon
2 × 411 g (14½ oz)
    cans chicken
    consommé
150 ml (¼ pint)
    double cream
pinch of cayenne
    pepper
2 drops Tabasco
    sauce
salt and white pepper
TO GARNISH:
lemon slices
parsley sprigs

Cut the avocados in half lengthwise, remove the stones and scoop out all the flesh. Mix with the lemon juice and sieve or work in an electric blender until smooth.

Transfer to a bowl and stir in the remaining ingredients, with salt and pepper to taste. Chill for several hours before serving.

Garnish with lemon slices and parsley sprigs. Serve with garlic and herb bread.

Serves 4 to 6

Prawn Bisque

25 g (1 oz) butter
1 onion, finely
    chopped
1 clove garlic,
    crushed
25 g (1 oz) plain
    flour
1 × 397 g (14 oz)
    and 1 × 227 g
    (8 oz) can tomatoes
juice of ½ lemon
1 bouquet garni
salt and pepper
2 tablespoons dry
    white wine
250 g (½ lb) cod or
    haddock fillets, cut
    into 2.5 cm
    (1 inch) pieces
250 g (8 oz) peeled
    prawns, roughly
    chopped

Melt the butter in a large pan, add the onion and garlic and cook for 5 minutes, without browning.

Stir in the flour and cook for 2 minutes. Gradually stir in the tomatoes, with their juice, and the lemon juice. Add the bouquet garni, and salt and pepper to taste. Bring to the boil, cover and simmer for 25 minutes.

Remove the bouquet garni. Sieve or work in an electric blender until smooth.

Return to the pan, stir in the wine, fish and prawns and cook for 5 to 7 minutes, until the fish is tender.

Transfer to a bowl and leave to cool, then chill for several hours before serving.

Serves 6

Chilled Almond Soup

15 g (½ oz) butter
1 small onion, finely
  chopped
25 g (1 oz) plain
  flour
900 ml (1½ pints)
  chicken stock
175 g (6 oz) flaked
  almonds
1 bay leaf
salt
150 ml (¼ pint)
  double cream
toasted flaked almonds
  to garnish

Melt the butter in a large pan, add the onion and cook for 5 minutes until transparent.

Stir in the flour and cook for 1 minute, without browning. Gradually add the stock, stirring constantly. Add the almonds, bay leaf and salt to taste. Bring to the boil, cover and simmer for 20 minutes.

Leave until cool, then remove the bay leaf. Sieve or work in an electric blender until smooth. Transfer to a bowl and chill for 2 to 3 hours.

Just before serving, stir in the cream and sprinkle over the toasted almonds.

Serves 4 to 6

Chilled Watercress Soup

25 g (1 oz) butter
2 leeks, thinly sliced
1 small onion,
    chopped
250 g (8 oz) potato,
    diced
2 bunches of
    watercress
600 ml (1 pint)
    chicken stock
salt and pepper
300 ml (½ pint)
    milk
croûtons to garnish

Melt the butter in a pan, add the leeks and onion and fry for 5 minutes, without browning. Add the potato and cook for 2 minutes.

Meanwhile, remove the tough stalks from the watercress and roughly chop the leaves. Add to the pan with the stock, and salt and pepper to taste. Bring to the boil, then cover and simmer for 25 to 30 minutes.

Sieve or work in an electric blender until smooth. Pour into a bowl and stir in the milk. Chill for several hours before serving.

Serve garnished with croûtons.
Serves 4 to 6

Summer Vegetable Soup

8 large ripe tomatoes
2 cloves garlic
½ small onion
½ cucumber
1 green pepper, cored
    and seeded
1 red pepper, cored
    and seeded
1 thyme sprig
1 basil sprig
2 parsley sprigs
6 tablespoons olive
    oil
4 tablespoons lemon
    juice
600 ml (1 pint)
    tomato juice,
    chilled
few drops of Tabasco
    sauce
TO SERVE:
garlic-flavoured
    croûtons
black olives
capers

Chop the tomatoes, garlic, onion, cucumber and peppers roughly. Put these ingredients into an electric blender and blend until smooth. Add the herbs and blend again.

Strain into a bowl and chill for several hours.

Just before serving, mix the olive oil and lemon juice together. Add the tomato juice and Tabasco, and gradually stir this mixture into the soup. Garnish with croûtons and serve black olives and capers as accompaniments.
Serves 6

Bortsch

4 large cooked
  beetroot
1.2 litres (2 pints)
  beef stock
2 large onions,
  roughly chopped
2 carrots, roughly
  chopped
1 celery stick,
  chopped
1 small strip of
  lemon peel
6 black peppercorns
1 bouquet garni
salt
1 tablespoon lemon
  juice
TO GARNISH:
garlic-flavoured
  croûtons
142 ml (5 fl oz)
  soured cream

Grate the beetroot and put in a large
pan with the stock, onions, carrots
and celery. Bring to the boil, add the
lemon peel, peppercorns, bouquet
garni, and salt to taste. Cover and
simmer for 35 to 40 minutes. Strain
into a soup tureen.

Leave to cool, then stir in the
lemon juice and chill for 2 to 3
hours.

Serve garnished with croûtons.
Hand the soured cream separately, or
stir into the soup before serving.
Serves 6 to 8

Prawn and Cucumber Soup

1 cucumber, peeled
  and diced
1 × 411 g (14½ oz)
  can chicken
  consommé
150 ml (¼ pint)
  tomato juice
150 g (5 oz) carton
  natural low-fat
  yogurt
150 ml (¼ pint)
  single cream
125 g (4 oz) peeled
  prawns, roughly
  chopped
2 drops Tabasco
  sauce
1 tablespoon chopped
  mint
1 clove garlic, crushed
salt and white pepper
TO GARNISH:
mint sprigs
cucumber slices

Place the cucumber in an electric blender and work until smooth. Transfer to a bowl and add the remaining ingredients, seasoning well with salt and pepper; mix well. Chill for several hours before serving.

    Garnish with mint and cucumber slices to serve.

Serves 4 to 6

HORS D'OEUVRE

For an hors d'oeuvre or antipasto course, serve 5 or 6 of the following – either on large platters for people to help themselves, or a little of each one on individual plates. Choose recipes which complement each other in flavour and colour.

Sauté of Aubergines

500 g (1 lb) aubergines
salt
3 tablespoons olive oil
2 cloves garlic, thinly sliced
2 tablespoons chopped parsley
TO GARNISH:
lime or lemon slices
parsley sprigs

Cut the aubergines into 1 cm (½ inch) pieces. Put into a colander, sprinkle generously with salt and leave for 30 minutes. Rinse well under cold water and drain on kitchen paper.

Heat the olive oil in a large frying pan, add the aubergines and fry for 10 to 12 minutes, until golden brown. Stir in the garlic and parsley and cook for a further 2 minutes.

Serve hot or cold, garnished with lime or lemon slices and parsley.
Serves 4 to 6

Courgette Appetizer

1 tablespoon oil
1 clove garlic, thinly
    sliced
1 small onion, finely
    chopped
300 ml (½ pint) dry
    white wine
1 bouquet garni
1 teaspoon cumin
    seeds
350 g (12 oz)
    courgettes, sliced
salt and pepper
2 tomatoes, skinned,
    seeded and chopped
chopped herbs to
    garnish

Heat the oil in a pan, add the garlic and onion and cook for 10 minutes, without browning.

Add the wine, bring to the boil and boil rapidly until reduced by half.

Add the bouquet garni, cumin seeds, courgettes, and salt and pepper to taste. Stir well and cook for 5 to 7 minutes, until the courgettes are just tender. Remove from the heat and stir in the tomatoes. Leave until cool.

Remove the bouquet garni and chill for at least 2 hours. Serve garnished with chopped herbs.
Serves 4 to 6

Rice, Tomato and Olive Salad

3 tablespoons long-
  grain rice
salt and pepper
4 tomatoes, skinned
50 g (2 oz) button
  mushrooms, thinly
  sliced
50 g (2 oz) black
  olives, stoned and
  halved
1 tablespoon chopped
  parsley
2 tablespoons olive oil
1 tablespoon lemon
  juice
½ clove garlic, crushed
1 teaspoon French
  mustard
2 teaspoons chopped
  basil
1 teaspoon caster
  sugar

Cook the rice in boiling salted water for 12 to 14 minutes, until tender. Drain and cool under cold running water, then drain again. Chop the tomatoes, discarding the seeds.

Put the rice, tomatoes, mushrooms and olives into a bowl and sprinkle over the parsley.

Mix the oil, lemon juice and garlic together. Blend in the mustard, basil, sugar, and salt and pepper to taste. Spoon the dressing over the rice mixture and mix well.

Transfer to a serving dish, cover and chill until required.
Serves 4 to 6

Artichokes Vinaigrette

1 × 397 g (14 oz) can
  artichoke hearts
2 hard-boiled eggs
DRESSING:
4 tablespoons olive
  oil
1 tablespoon lemon
  juice
1 teaspoon finely
  grated lemon rind
1 tablespoon white
  wine
1 teaspoon clear
  honey
1 tablespoon each
  chopped parsley,
  oregano, thyme
  and basil
TO GARNISH:
1 tablespoon capers

Rinse the artichokes under cold running water and drain well. Cut each piece into quarters. Cut the eggs into quarters. Arrange the eggs and artichokes on a serving plate.

Mix all the dressing ingredients together, stirring well so that the herbs are evenly distributed.

Spoon the dressing over the salad and sprinkle with the capers. Cover and chill until required.
Serves 4 to 6

Peppers en Salade

2 each red, green and
  yellow peppers
4 tablespoons olive
  oil
2 tablespoons wine
  vinegar
1 teaspoon caster
  sugar
salt and pepper
1 teaspoon Meaux
  mustard
1 × 50 g (1¾ oz)
  can anchovy
  fillets, drained
black olives to
  garnish

Preheat the grill to very hot. Grill the
peppers as close to the heat as
possible until the skin is charred on
all sides. Rub off the skins under cold
running water.

Halve the peppers and remove the
cores and seeds. Slice into thin strips
and arrange on a plate.

Mix the oil, vinegar and sugar
together with salt and pepper to
taste. Add the mustard and mix well.

Spoon the dressing over the
peppers. Arrange the anchovy fillets
in a lattice pattern over the top and
garnish with olives.

Cover and chill until required.
Serves 4 to 6

Cold Meat Platter

125 g (4 oz) garlic
    sausage, thinly
    sliced
125 g (4 oz) Italian
    or German salami,
    thinly sliced
6-8 slices Parma
    ham, or other raw
    smoked ham,
    thinly sliced
6-8 slices honey roast
    ham, thinly sliced
6-8 slices cooked
    tongue, thinly
    sliced
TO GARNISH:
radishes and olives,
    or figs

Arrange the garlic sausage, salami,
hams and tongue on a serving platter
and garnish with radishes and olives,
or figs.

Serve with a selection of salads.

Serves 6 to 8

NOTE: In Italy a cold platter such as
this is often served with slices of
melon, fresh figs and bread sticks.

Mixed Vegetable Salad

2 tablespoons olive oil
1-2 cloves garlic,
    crushed
8 button onions
2 courgettes, sliced
125 g (4 oz) button
    mushrooms
few cauliflower
    florets
2 celery sticks,
    chopped
1 × 397 g (14 oz)
    can tomatoes
6 coriander seeds
1 bouquet garni
4 tablespoons dry
    white wine
1 tablespoon green
    peppercorns
    (optional)
salt
coriander or parsley
    sprigs to garnish

Heat the oil in a pan, add the garlic
and cook for 2 minutes, without
browning. Stir in the onions,
courgettes, mushrooms, cauliflower
and celery.

Add the tomatoes with their juice
and bring to the boil. Add the
coriander seeds, bouquet garni,
wine, peppercorns if using, and salt
to taste. Simmer rapidly for 15 to 20
minutes, until the vegetables are just
tender and the liquid reduced.
Discard the bouquet garni and leave
to cool.

Spoon into a serving dish and chill
until required. Garnish with
coriander or parsley to serve.

Serves 4 to 6

NOTE: If green peppercorns are
omitted, add freshly ground black
pepper to taste.

Mushrooms Italienne

4 shelled scallops
4 tablespoons dry
    white wine
1 parsley sprig
¼ small onion
strip of lemon rind
125 g (4 oz) peeled
    prawns
250 g (8 oz) button
    mushrooms, thinly
    sliced
6 tablespoons olive oil
2 tablespoons lemon
    or lime juice
½ clove garlic, crushed
1 teaspoon chopped
    parsley
salt and pepper
few lettuce leaves
TO GARNISH:
parsley sprigs
lime or lemon slices

Separate the coral from the white scallop meat then slice the scallops.

Put the wine, parsley sprig, onion and lemon rind into a pan, add the scallops and cook for 2 minutes.

Using a slotted spoon, lift out the fish and put into a bowl. Leave to cool, then stir in the prawns.

Put the mushrooms into another bowl and pour over the oil and lemon or lime juice. Sprinkle with the garlic, parsley and plenty of pepper. Toss well and leave to stand for 30 minutes. Stir in a little salt, add to the fish and stir well.

Arrange the lettuce leaves on individual serving dishes and pile the mushroom mixture on top. Cover and chill until required.

Garnish with parsley and lime or lemon slices to serve.

Serves 4 to 6

44

Crispy Cheese Fries

50 g (2 oz) butter
50 g (2 oz) plain
flour
450 ml (¾ pint)
milk
salt and pepper
freshly grated nutmeg
175 g (6 oz) Gruyère
cheese, grated
2 tablespoons grated
Parmesan cheese
1 × 177 g (6 oz)
can crabmeat,
drained and flaked
2 egg yolks, beaten
1 egg
2 tablespoons milk
fresh breadcrumbs for
coating
oil for deep-frying
fried parsley sprigs to
garnish

Melt the butter in a pan, stir in the flour and cook for 2 minutes. Gradually add the milk, stirring constantly. Bring to the boil, and add salt, pepper and nutmeg to taste. Add the cheeses and stir until melted.

Remove from the heat and mix in the crabmeat and egg yolks. Spread the mixture in a shallow baking tin to a 1 cm (½ inch) thickness. Cover with foil and chill for 3 to 4 hours.

Cut the paste into rectangles, about 4 cm (1½ inches) long. Beat the egg with the milk. Dip the cheese cubes into the egg mixture, then into the breadcrumbs to coat evenly. Heat the oil in a deep-fryer to 190°C (375°F) and fry the cheese cubes in batches until crisp and golden.

Serve hot, garnished with fried parsley.

Serves 6

Tomatoes with Fresh Herbs

4 tablespoons
  chopped parsley
2 tablespoons each
  chopped basil and
  tarragon
2 tablespoons finely
  chopped onion
2 spring onions,
  finely chopped
1 clove garlic, crushed
6 tablespoons olive oil
3 tablespoons wine
  vinegar
1 teaspoon clear
  honey
salt and pepper
8 large ripe tomatoes,
  skinned and sliced

Mix the herbs, onions and garlic together, then gradually add the oil, vinegar and honey to form a thick sauce. Season well with salt and pepper.

Arrange a layer of tomatoes on a serving platter and spoon over some dressing. Put another layer of tomatoes on top and spoon over more dressing. Continue with these layers until all the ingredients are used. Cover and chill for 30 minutes.
Serves 4 to 6

Tuscan Bean Salad

1 × 425 g (15 oz)
  can cannellini
  beans, drained
1 × 425 g (15 oz)
  can green flageolet
  or broad beans,
  drained
1 small onion, thinly
  sliced
6 tablespoons olive
  oil
25 g (1 oz) black
  olives, stoned
1 tablespoon chopped
  parsley
1 tablespoon chopped
  oregano or
  marjoram
1 × 198 g (7 oz)
  can tuna fish,
  drained
salt and pepper
2 radichio or chicory
  heads to serve

Mix the beans together in a bowl. Stir in the onion, oil, olives and herbs. Flake the tuna and add to the salad. Toss well and season with salt and pepper to taste.

Arrange the radichio leaves or chicory on a serving platter. Spoon the bean salad on top. Cover and chill until required.
Serves 4 to 6

Eggs with Piquant Mayonnaise

6 tablespoons thick
  mayonnaise
1 tablespoon lemon
  juice
½ clove garlic, crushed
2 tablespoons
  chopped parsley
1 tablespoon each
  chopped tarragon
  and basil
2 tablespoons capers
2 × 50 g (1¾ oz)
  cans anchovy
  fillets, drained
pepper
6 eggs, hard-boiled
1 curly endive

Put the mayonnaise and lemon juice
into a bowl. Mix in the garlic, herbs
and 1 tablespoon capers. Chop half
of the anchovy fillets very finely and
add to the mayonnaise. Season with
pepper to taste.

Cut the eggs in half lengthways.
Place the curly endive leaves on
individual serving plates and arrange
the eggs on top, cut side down.
Spoon the herb mayonnaise over and
arrange the remaining anchovy fillets
in a lattice pattern over each egg.
Top with the remaining capers.

Serve chilled.

Serves 6

FRUIT & VEGETABLE STARTERS

Charentais Melon with Grapes

2 large even-sized
  Charentais melons
250 g (8 oz) small
  green grapes
150 ml (¼ pint)
  white wine
4 pieces of stem
  ginger chopped
caster sugar

Cut the melons in half and scoop out the flesh with a melon baller, or cut into cubes. Place in a bowl. Reserve the shells.

Skin the grapes, halve and remove the pips. Add the grapes to the bowl and pour over the wine, then add the chopped ginger and sugar to taste. Mix well, cover and chill for 2 hours.

Spoon the mixture into the melon shells and serve immediately.

Serves 4

Pears with Tarragon Mayonnaise

150 ml (¼ pint)
  thick mayonnaise
4 tablespoons single
  cream
2 teaspoons tarragon
  wine vinegar
salt
cayenne pepper
2 tablespoons
  chopped tarragon
few lettuce leaves
4 ripe Comice or
  William pears
lemon twists to
  garnish

Put the mayonnaise, cream and vinegar into a bowl, with salt and cayenne pepper to taste. Stir in the chopped tarragon and mix well. Cover and set aside.

Arrange the lettuce leaves on 4 individual plates. Peel the pears and scoop out the cores with a teaspoon. Place one pear on each plate. Spoon over the tarragon mayonnaise and garnish with lemon twists. Serve chilled.

Serves 4

Waldorf Salad

juice of 1 lemon
500 g (1 lb) red
    dessert apples,
    cored and sliced
1 head of celery,
    sliced
150 ml (¼ pint)
    mayonnaise
1 teaspoon caster
    sugar
75 g (3 oz) walnuts,
    roughly chopped
1 crisp lettuce

Put the lemon juice in a large mixing bowl, add the apples and toss quickly to prevent them discolouring. Set aside a few apple slices for garnish.

Add the celery, mayonnaise, sugar and walnuts to the bowl and mix well; make sure all the ingredients are thoroughly combined.

Arrange the lettuce in a salad bowl and pile the salad on top. Garnish with the reserved apple slices and serve immediately.
Serves 4 to 6

Citrus and Chicory Salad

4 heads of chicory
3 oranges
2 limes or 1 grapefruit
4 tablespoons olive oil
2 tablespoons lemon
    juice
1 teaspoon French
    mustard
salt and pepper
2 teaspoons chopped
    parsley
few lettuce leaves
lime or orange slices
    to garnish

Slice the chicory into rings and put into a bowl. Peel the oranges and limes or grapefruit and cut into segments, discarding all the pith. Add to the chicory.

Blend the oil, lemon juice and mustard together. Season with salt and pepper to taste and stir in the parsley. Pour over the salad and toss well.

Arrange the lettuce in a salad bowl and pile the salad on top. Garnish with lime or orange slices to serve.
Serves 4

Honeydew Melon Salad

500 g (1 lb) tomatoes
1 ripe Honeydew
    melon, peeled
1 cucumber
4 tablespoons olive
    oil
2 tablespoons lemon
    juice
1 tablespoon each
    chopped tarragon,
    parsley and chives
salt and pepper
few lettuce leaves

Set aside a few tomato slices for garnish. Skin and chop the remainder, discarding the seeds. Dice the melon and cucumber. Combine the melon, cucumber and tomatoes in a bowl.

Blend together the oil, lemon juice, herbs, and salt and pepper to taste. Spoon over the salad and mix well. Cover and chill for 2 to 3 hours. Arrange the lettuce in a bowl and pile the salad on top. Garnish with the tomato slices to serve.
Serves 6

Melon and Mint Refresher

175 g (6 oz) caster
    sugar
5 tablespoons water
small bunch of mint
1 large ripe melon
grated rind and juice
    of 2 limes or
    lemons
2 egg whites
mint sprigs to garnish

Put the sugar and water in a pan and heat until dissolved, stirring. Bring to the boil and simmer for about 10 minutes. Add the mint and mix well. Allow to cool.

Cut the melon flesh into chunks and purée in an electric blender. Strain the mint flavoured syrup onto the melon and add the lime or lemon rind and juice. Pour into a rigid freezerproof container, cover, seal and freeze for 2 to 3 hours, until half frozen but still soft in the centre.

Turn into a bowl and beat until smooth. Whisk the egg whites until stiff, then fold into the melon mixture. Return to the container, cover, seal and freeze until firm.

Transfer to the refrigerator 30 minutes before required, to soften slightly. Scoop into chilled individual serving dishes and garnish with mint sprigs to serve.
Serves 6

Apple and Ginger Sorbet

4 cooking apples,
    peeled, cored and
    sliced
grated rind and juice
    of ½ lemon
3 tablespoons soft
    brown sugar
1 teaspoon ground
    ginger
6 pieces of stem
    ginger, diced
4 tablespoons ginger
    syrup (from stem
    ginger jar)
150 ml (¼ pint)
    apple juice
2 egg whites
stem ginger slices to
    garnish

Cook the apples with the lemon rind and juice until very soft. Sieve, then stir in the sugar and ground ginger and leave to cool.

Stir in the stem ginger, ginger syrup and apple juice and mix well. Pour into a rigid freezerproof container, cover, seal and freeze for about 1 hour, until the mixture is half-frozen and mushy.

Turn into a bowl and beat until smooth. Whisk the egg whites until stiff, then fold into the apple mixture. Freeze until firm.

Transfer to the refrigerator about 30 minutes before required to soften slightly. Scoop into chilled dishes and top with ginger slices.
Serves 6

Tomato and Basil Sorbet

1 × 1.2 litre
   (43 fl oz) can
   tomato juice
juice of ½ lemon
1 tablespoon
   Worcestershire
   sauce
2 teaspoons finely
   chopped basil
2 tablespoons dry
   white wine
2 drops Tabasco
   sauce
salt and pepper
2 egg whites
basil leaves to
   garnish

Mix the tomato juice, lemon juice,
Worcestershire sauce, basil, wine and
Tabasco together. Season with salt
and pepper to taste.

Pour into a rigid freezerproof
container, cover, seal and freeze for
about 1½ hours, until mushy.

Turn into a bowl and whisk well.
Return to the container and freeze for
a further 1 hour, then whisk again.
Whisk the egg whites until stiff, then
fold into the tomato mixture. Freeze
until firm.

Transfer to the refrigerator
30 minutes before required to soften
slightly. Spoon into chilled
individual dishes and serve garnished
with basil.

Serves 6 to 8

Stuffed Pear Hors d'Oeuvre

113 g (4 oz) cream
  cheese
1 tablespoon chopped
  chives
2 teaspoons chopped
  parsley
25 g (1 oz) walnuts,
  chopped
1 apple, peeled,
  cored and grated
2 teaspoons lemon
  juice
1 head of chicory
4 large ripe pears
4 slices raw smoked
  ham

Beat the cream cheese until soft. Mix in the herbs and nuts, then fold in the apple and lemon juice.

Arrange the chicory leaves on 4 individual serving plates. Peel the pears, halve and remove the cores. Spoon the filling into the core cavities and arrange two halves on each plate.

Roll up the ham slices and place in the centre. Serve immediately.

Serves 4

Prosciutto con Fichi

12 very thin slices
  Parma ham, or
  other raw smoked
  ham
1 Ogen melon,
  seeded and cut into
  4 wedges
8 ripe figs

Divide the ham between 4 individual plates and top with the melon.

Cut the figs into sections, from the stem end nearly through to the base, taking care not to cut right through. Peel back the skin and put 2 'flower' figs on either side of each melon wedge. Serve immediately.

Serves 4

Guacamole

2 ripe avocados
1 clove garlic, crushed
½ onion, chopped
1 tablespoon lime
  juice
2 drops Tabasco
  sauce
4 tomatoes, skinned,
  seeded and chopped
2 tablespoons
  chopped parsley
salt and pepper
1 teaspoon chilli
  powder
lime slices to garnish

Peel, halve and stone the avocados. Purée in an electric blender, with the garlic, onion, lime juice, Tabasco, tomatoes and parsley, until smooth. Season liberally with salt and pepper, add the chilli powder and blend again until thoroughly mixed.

Pile into a serving dish and chill for 1 hour. Garnish with lime slices and serve with melba toast or brown bread.

Serves 4 to 6

NOTE: Do not chill for more than 1 hour or the guacamole may discolour.

Prawn Stuffed Courgettes

8 small, even-sized
  courgettes
salt and pepper
1 tablespoon oil
1 clove garlic, crushed
2 shallots, finely
  chopped
4 tomatoes, skinned,
  seeded and chopped
2 drops Tabasco
  sauce
1 teaspoon crumbled
  thyme
250 g (8 oz) peeled
  prawns
25 g (1 oz) butter
25 g (1 oz) plain flour
300 ml (½ pint)
  milk
1 teaspoon made
  mustard
125 g (4 oz) Cheddar
  cheese, grated
1 tablespoon grated
  Parmesan cheese

Blanch the courgettes in boiling salted water for 2 minutes, drain and cool quickly. Halve lengthways, scoop out the flesh and chop. Arrange the shells in a shallow ovenproof dish.

Heat the oil in a pan, add the garlic and shallots and cook gently for 5 minutes. Add the tomatoes, courgette flesh, Tabasco, thyme, and salt and pepper to taste. Bring to the boil and cook, uncovered, for 25 minutes, stirring occasionally.

Add the prawns, then spoon the sauce into and over the courgettes.

Melt the butter in a pan, stir in the flour and cook for 1 minute. Gradually stir in the milk. Bring to the boil and cook, stirring, for 2 minutes. Stir in the mustard, cheeses and salt and pepper to taste.

Spoon over the courgettes and bake in a preheated hot oven, 220°C (425°F), Gas Mark 7, for 15 to 20 minutes, until golden. Serve immediately.
Serves 6 to 8

Avocado with Curried Sauce

2 ripe avocados
juice of ½ lemon
SAUCE:
*1-2 teaspoons curry
    powder*
1 clove garlic, crushed
*150 ml (¼ pint)
    mayonnaise*
*150 ml (¼ pint)
    double cream*
*2 drops Tabasco
    sauce*
salt and pepper
*2 hard-boiled eggs,
    chopped*
*1 tablespoon chopped
    parsley*
TO GARNISH:
lemon twists
*parsley or basil
    leaves*

First, make the sauce. Put the curry
powder and garlic in a bowl and
gradually mix in the mayonnaise and
cream. Add the Tabasco sauce and
season with salt and pepper to taste.
Cover and leave in the refrigerator
for 4 to 6 hours to allow the flavour
to mellow.

Add the chopped eggs and parsley
to the sauce and stir well.

Cut the avocados in half, remove
the stones and sprinkle with lemon
juice.

Arrange the avocado halves on
4 individual plates. Spoon the sauce
into each avocado and serve
immediately, garnished with lemon
twists and parsley or basil leaves.
Serves 4

Marinated Mushrooms

4 tablespoons oil
2 cloves garlic,
   crushed
1 small onion, finely
   chopped
2 bay leaves
1 thyme sprig
1 rosemary sprig
2 parsley sprigs
200 ml (⅓ pint) dry
   white wine
4-6 peppercorns
12 coriander seeds
750 g (1½ lb)
   button mushrooms
salt
chopped parsley to
   garnish

Heat the oil in a pan, add the garlic and onion and cook for 10 minutes, without browning. Stir in the herbs and wine, bring to the boil and simmer for 2 minutes. Add the peppercorns, coriander seeds, mushrooms, and salt to taste. Toss the mushrooms in the wine sauce until well coated.

Transfer to a bowl, cover and chill for 3 to 4 hours, stirring occasionally.

Spoon into a serving dish and sprinkle over the parsley. Serve with French bread or granary rolls.
Serves 6

Crispy Mushrooms with Herb and Garlic Mayonnaise

500 g (1 lb) button
  mushrooms
oil for deep-frying
BATTER:
125 g (4 oz) plain
  flour
pinch of salt
1 tablespoon oil
150 ml (¼ pint) water
2 egg whites
MAYONNAISE:
8 tablespoons
  mayonnaise
1-2 cloves garlic,
  crushed
2 tablespoons
  chopped parsley
1 tablespoon chopped
  basil

First, make the batter. Sift the flour
and salt into a bowl, then gradually
beat in the oil and water. Whisk the
egg whites until very stiff, then fold
into the batter.

Drop the mushrooms into the
batter. Heat the oil in a deep-fryer to
190°C (375°F). Deep-fry the
mushrooms in batches, lifting them
from the batter to the oil, using a
slotted spoon. Drain on kitchen
paper and keep hot while frying the
remaining mushrooms.

Mix the mayonnaise ingredients
together and spoon into a bowl.
Serve immediately, with the hot
mushrooms.
Serves 4 to 6

Broad Beans à la Grecque

2 tablespoons oil
1 clove garlic, thinly
  sliced
1 onion, finely
  chopped
500 g (1 lb) shelled
  broad beans
8 tomatoes, skinned,
  seeded and chopped
2 tablespoons dry
  white wine
1 tablespoon chopped
  parsley
1 bay leaf
salt and pepper

Heat the oil in a pan, add the garlic
and onion and fry for 4 to 5 minutes,
without browning.

Stir in the broad beans and toss
well to coat in the oil. Add the
remaining ingredients, with salt and
pepper to taste. Bring to the boil,
cover and simmer for 15 minutes or
until the beans are tender. Remove
the bay leaf and leave to cool.

Serve chilled, with brown bread.

Serves 4

NOTE: Frozen broad beans can be
used: cook the tomato mixture for
10 minutes before adding them.

Aubergine Cheesecake   *very good*

350 g (12 oz)
  aubergines, diced
salt and pepper
50 g (2 oz) butter
125 g (4 oz)
  Cheddar cheese
  biscuits, crushed
1 tablespoon grated
  Parmesan cheese
4 tablespoons oil
1 onion, thinly sliced
1 × 227 g (8 oz)
  packet cream
  cheese, softened
142 ml (5 fl oz)
  soured cream
½ teaspoon dried
  mixed herbs
3 eggs, beaten
175 g (6 oz)
  Cheddar cheese,
  grated

Put the aubergines in a large
colander, sprinkle generously with
salt and leave to drain for 1 hour.

Melt the butter in a pan over low
heat. Remove from the heat and stir
in the crushed biscuits and Parmesan
cheese. Press into the base of a
greased 20 cm (8 inch) loose-
bottomed cake tin.

Heat the oil in a pan, add the
onion and fry until lightly browned.
Remove with a slotted spoon and set
aside.

Rinse the aubergines under cold
water, drain and dry on kitchen
paper. Add to the pan and fry until
lightly coloured. Drain thoroughly.

Blend the cream cheese and soured
cream together, adding salt and
pepper to taste. Stir in the herbs,
eggs and Cheddar cheese. Add the
onions and aubergines and mix well.

Spread over the biscuit base and
bake in a preheated moderately hot
oven, 190°C (375°F), Gas Mark 5, for
35 to 40 minutes, until set and
golden brown. Serve hot or cold.

Serves 6 to 8

Philadelphia full fat.

60   *(30 mins 8/11) (60 mins 10/12)*

Leek Soufflé

50 g (2 oz) butter
500 g (1 lb) leeks,
   thinly sliced
25 g (1 oz) plain
   flour
150 ml (¼ pint)
   milk
125 g (4 oz)
   matured Cheddar
   cheese, grated
1 tablespoon grated
   Parmesan cheese
1 teaspoon made
   mustard
salt and pepper
6 eggs, separated

Melt half the butter in a pan, add the leeks and toss until coated in butter. Cook for 5 to 7 minutes until soft.

Melt the remaining butter in another pan, stir in the flour and cook for 1 minute. Gradually add the milk, stirring constantly. Cook, stirring, for 1 minute then add the cheeses, mustard, and salt and pepper to taste. Stir until the cheeses have melted. Remove from the heat and leave to cool for 5 minutes, then beat in the egg yolks. Drain the leeks, then stir into the sauce.

Whisk the egg whites until very stiff, then carefully fold into the leek mixture. Turn into a greased 1.2 litre (2 pint) soufflé dish and bake in a preheated moderate oven, 180°C (350°F), Gas Mark 4, for 45 minutes, until well risen and golden brown.

Serve immediately.

Serves 4 to 6

Aubergine Pie

500 g (1 lb)
    aubergines, sliced
salt and pepper
3 tablespoons oil
250 g (8 oz) Mozza-
    rella cheese, sliced
1 tablespoon grated
    Parmesan cheese
2 tablespoons
    breadcrumbs
TOMATO SAUCE:
1 tablespoon oil
1 clove garlic, crushed
1 large onion, chopped
500 g (1 lb)
    tomatoes, skinned,
    seeded and chopped
1 bouquet garni
3 tablespoons dry
    white wine
1 teaspoon Worcester-
    shire sauce
1 tablespoon tomato
    purée

Sprinkle the aubergines with salt, place in a colander and leave for 1 hour. Rinse in cold water and dry on kitchen paper.

Meanwhile, make the sauce. Heat the oil in a pan, add the garlic and onion and sauté until soft. Add the tomatoes and cook for 2 minutes. Add the remaining ingredients, with salt and pepper to taste. Simmer, uncovered, for 45 minutes, until thickened. Remove bouquet garni.

Heat the oil in a frying pan, add the aubergine slices and fry until golden. Drain on kitchen paper.

Fill a shallow ovenproof dish with alternate layers of aubergines, Mozzarella and tomato sauce, finishing with cheese. Sprinkle with Parmesan and breadcrumbs.

Bake in a preheated moderately hot oven, 200°C (400°F), Gas Mark 6, for 30 minutes. Serve hot or cold.
Serves 6 to 8

French Tomato Tartlets

SHORTCRUST PASTRY:

250 g (8 oz) plain flour
pinch of salt
50 g (2 oz) lard
50 g (2 oz) butter
25 g (1 oz) grated Parmesan cheese
1-2 tablespoons iced water

FILLING:

25 g (1 oz) butter
2 onions, sliced
350 g (12 oz) tomatoes, skinned and thickly sliced
12 anchovy fillets, soaked in a little milk for 10 minutes then drained
24 black olives
1-2 tablespoons oil

To make the pastry, sift the flour and salt into a mixing bowl, then rub in the lard and butter until the mixture resembles fine breadcrumbs. Stir in the cheese, then mix in sufficient water to make a firm dough. Cover and chill for 15 minutes. Knead lightly, roll out on a floured board and use to line six 7.5 cm (3 inch) individual tins. Prick the base of each case. Chill for 30 minutes.

Melt the butter in a pan, add the onions and cook until lightly browned. Cool, then sprinkle over the base of the pastry cases. Place the tomatoes on top, then arrange 2 anchovy fillets in a cross on top and place an olive in each quarter. Sprinkle a little oil over each tart.

Bake in a preheated moderate oven, 180°C (350°F), Gas Mark 4, for 25 to 30 minutes, until the pastry is golden.

Serve hot or cold.

Serves 6

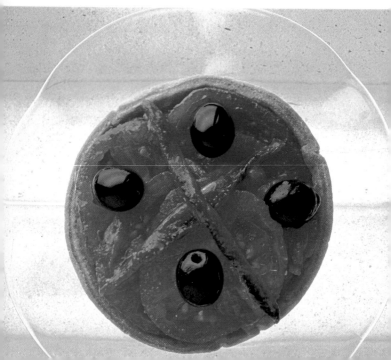

Ratatouille Tartlets

SHORTCRUST
  PASTRY:
250 g (8 oz) plain
  flour
pinch of salt
50 g (2 oz) lard
50 g (2 oz) butter
1-2 tablespoons iced
  water
RATATOUILLE:
15 g (½ oz) butter
1 clove garlic, sliced
1 onion, sliced
1 small aubergine,
  chopped
1 courgette, sliced
4 tomatoes, skinned,
  seeded and chopped
1 tablespoon tomato
  purée
salt and pepper
TO SERVE:
Parmesan cheese
  (optional)

Make the pastry and chill as for
French Tomato Tartlets (opposite),
omitting the cheese. Knead lightly,
then roll out on a floured board and
use to line six 7.5 cm (3 inch)
individual flan tins. Prick the bases.
Chill for 30 minutes.

Melt the butter in a pan, add the
garlic and onion and cook gently for
10 minutes. Stir in the aubergine,
courgette, tomatoes, tomato purée,
and salt and pepper to taste. Cover
and simmer for 20 minutes.

Line the pastry cases with foil or
greaseproof paper and beans and
bake in a preheated moderately hot
oven, 200°C (400°F), Gas Mark 6, for
12 minutes, until golden brown.
Remove the paper and beans and
cook for a further 5 minutes.

Spoon the ratatouille into the flan
cases and sprinkle with Parmesan if
liked. Serve hot or cold.
Serves 6

Trout with Ham and Garlic

4 slices Parma ham
  or other raw
  smoked ham, fat
  removed
4 trout, cleaned, with
  heads and tails
  intact
salt and pepper
4 tablespoons olive
  oil
2 cloves garlic, thinly
  sliced
grated rind and juice
  of 1 lemon
2 tablespoons
  chopped parsley
TO GARNISH:
lemon wedges
parsley sprigs

Roll up the ham and place one piece inside the cavity of each trout. Season each fish liberally with salt and pepper.

Heat the oil in a frying pan, add the garlic and 2 trout and fry for 5 to 8 minutes on each side, until cooked. Drain on kitchen paper and keep hot while cooking the other trout. Add the lemon rind and juice to the pan and cook for 1 minute.

Arrange the trout on warmed dishes and spoon over the garlic and lemon flavoured oil. Sprinkle with the chopped parsley and serve immediately, garnished with lemon wedges and parsley sprigs.
Serves 4

Mussel Antipasto

1.75 kg (4 lb) mussels in shells, scrubbed clean

3 cloves garlic, crushed

2 teaspoons grated lemon rind

3 tablespoons chopped parsley

1 basil sprig, chopped

2 thyme sprigs, chopped

40 g (1½ oz) fresh white breadcrumbs

5 tablespoons olive oil

parsley sprigs to garnish

Cook the mussels in a pan containing 300 ml (½ pint) boiling water for about 5 minutes, until the shells have opened; discard any that do not. Drain.

Discard the empty half shell from each mussel. Arrange the mussels in their half shells in a large shallow flameproof dish, or individual dishes.

Mix the garlic, lemon rind, herbs and breadcrumbs together and sprinkle over the mussels. Spoon over the oil and place under a preheated moderate grill for 5 to 7 minutes, until pale golden; do not overcook or the mussels will become tough.

Serve immediately, garnished with parsley.

Serves 4 to 6

Mussels in Curry Sauce

1.75 kg (4 lb)
  mussels in shells
25 g (1 oz) butter
1 small onion, finely
  chopped
1 teaspoon curry
  powder
1 teaspoon tomato
  purée
4 tablespoons dry
  white wine
2 tablespoons apricot
  jam, sieved
salt and pepper
150 ml (¼ pint)
  double cream
150 ml (¼ pint)
  mayonnaise
juice of ½ lemon
TO SERVE:
350 g (12 oz) cooked
  long-grain rice,
  cooled
parsley sprigs

Scrub the mussels clean, then cook in a pan containing 300 ml (½ pint) boiling water for about 5 minutes, until the shells have opened; discard any that do not; drain. Reserve a few for garnish and remove the rest of the mussels from their shells.

Melt the butter in a pan, add the onion and sauté for 2 to 3 minutes. Stir in the curry powder and fry for a few minutes, then stir in the tomato purée, wine, apricot jam, and salt and pepper to taste.

Allow the sauce to cool. Lightly whip the cream, then fold into the sauce with the mayonnaise and lemon juice. Cover and chill for 2 to 3 hours, then fold in the shelled mussels.

Arrange the rice on individual serving dishes and spoon the mussel mixture into the centre. Garnish with the mussels and parsley to serve.
Serves 4 to 6

Insalata di Mare

4 squid
4-6 shelled scallops,
    quartered
12 mussels in shells,
    scrubbed clean
250 g (8 oz) peeled
    prawns
1 × 177 g (6 oz)
    can crabmeat,
    drained
4 tablespoons olive
    oil
2 tablespoons lemon
    juice
1 clove garlic, crushed
2 tablespoons
    chopped parsley
salt and pepper
lemon slices to
    garnish

Discard the ink sacs from the squid and cut the fish into small pieces.

Cook the scallops in a pan containing 300 ml (½ pint) boiling water for 2 to 3 minutes. Remove with a slotted spoon and set aside.

Add the squid to the pan and cook for 15 minutes, until tender. Remove with a slotted spoon and set aside.

Add the mussels to the pan and cook for about 5 minutes until the shells have opened; discard any that do not open. Drain and remove the top shell from each mussel.

Put all the fish into a bowl. Mix the oil, lemon juice, garlic and parsley together, adding salt and pepper to taste. Pour over the fish and toss well to coat. Cover and chill for 30 minutes.

Garnish with lemon slices and serve with brown bread.
Serves 4 to 6

Grilled Crab

4 small cooked crabs
juice of ½ lemon
25 g (1 oz) butter
1 small onion, finely
    chopped
120 ml (4 fl oz) dry
    sherry
1 teaspoon Worcester-
    shire sauce
1 teaspoon French
    mustard
1 teaspoon crumbled
    thyme
2 teaspoons chopped
    parsley
284 ml (10 fl oz)
    double cream
salt and pepper
2 tablespoons fresh
    breadcrumbs
1 tablespoon grated
    Parmesan cheese
4 whole prawns to
    garnish (optional)

Twist off the claws and legs from the
crabs, crack open and extract all the
meat. Remove the white and brown
meat from the body shells, discarding
the grey sac and feathered gills.

Flake the crabmeat into a basin and
add the lemon juice. Scrub the crab
shells and set aside.

Melt the butter in a pan, add the
onion and cook until golden. Pour in
the sherry and cook rapidly until the
liquid is reduced by two thirds.

Stir in the Worcestershire sauce,
mustard and herbs. Pour in the
cream and cook until thickened, then
stir in the crab meat. Season with salt
and pepper to taste.

Spoon into the crab shells and
sprinkle with the breadcrumbs and
Parmesan cheese. Cook under a
preheated moderate grill until
bubbling and golden brown. Serve
hot, garnished with prawns if liked.
Serves 4

Fritto Misto di Mare

4 squid
6 king-size prawns,
    peeled
2 fillets plaice or
    sole, cut into 5 cm
    (2 inch) strips
oil for deep-frying
BATTER:
125 g (4 oz) plain
    flour
pinch of salt
2 tablespoons olive
    oil
150 ml (¼ pint)
    water
1 large egg white,
    stiffly whisked
TO GARNISH:
lemon slices
fried parsley

Remove the ink sacs from the squid
and cut the flesh into small pieces.
Place in a pan of boiling water and
cook for 2 minutes. Drain and dry
on kitchen paper. Set aside with the
prawns and plaice or sole.

To make the batter, sift the flour
and salt into a bowl, gradually add
the oil and water, then fold in the
egg white.

Heat the oil in a deep-fryer to
190°C (375°F). Dip each type of fish
in turn into the batter, drain off any
excess, then fry in the hot oil until
golden brown. Drain on kitchen
paper and keep hot while frying the
remaining fish.

Arrange the fritto misto on a
warmed serving dish. Garnish with
lemon slices and parsley.
Serves 6

Cheese and Shrimp Soufflés

2 large eggs
150 ml (¼ pint)
 single cream
1 teaspoon English
 mustard
pinch of cayenne
 pepper
salt
75 g (3 oz) peeled
 shrimps
125 g (4 oz) matured
 Cheddar cheese,
 finely grated
1 tablespoon grated
 Parmesan cheese
ANCHOVY PASTE:
2 × 50 g (1¾ oz)
 cans anchovy fillets
4 tablespoons milk
1 tablespoon oil
2 cloves garlic, crushed
1 tablespoon chopped
 parsley
TO SERVE:
French bread

For the anchovy paste, drain the
anchovy fillets and soak them in the
milk for 30 minutes. Rinse
thoroughly in cold water and drain.

Pound the anchovies with the oil,
garlic and parsley to a smooth paste.
Keep on one side.

Beat together the eggs, cream,
mustard, cayenne, and salt to taste.
Stir in the shrimps and cheeses.

Lightly grease four individual
soufflé dishes and pour in the
mixture. Bake in a preheated
moderately hot oven, 200°C (400°F),
Gas Mark 6, for 20 to 25 minutes,
until well risen and golden brown.

Meanwhile toast the French bread
on both sides. Spread with the
prepared anchovy paste and heat
through under a preheated moderate
grill. Arrange on a warmed serving
platter. Serve the soufflés as soon as
they are cooked, with the anchovy
toasts.
Serves 4

Prawn Pilaff

50 g (2 oz) butter
1 small onion, finely
  chopped
1 clove garlic, crushed
250 g (8 oz) long-
  grain rice
200 ml (⅓ pint) dry
  white wine
2-3 strands of saffron
600 ml (1 pint) fish
  or chicken stock
  (approximately)
salt and pepper
4 tomatoes, skinned,
  seeded and chopped
1 tablespoon chopped
  basil
250 g (8 oz) peeled
  prawns
TO GARNISH:
basil leaves
few whole prawns
  (optional)

Melt the butter in a pan, add the onion and garlic and cook gently for 5 minutes. Add the rice and toss until coated in the butter. Add the wine and saffron and bring to the boil, stirring. Cook until most of the wine has evaporated, stirring constantly.

Stir in two thirds of the stock and season with salt and pepper to taste. Bring to the boil, cover and simmer for 10 to 12 minutes until the rice is just tender, stirring occasionally; add more stock if required, to keep the rice slightly moist and ensure it does not burn. Stir in the tomatoes, basil and prawns and cook for 2 minutes.

Pile the pilaff into a warmed serving dish. Garnish with basil and whole prawns if using. Serve with Parmesan cheese.
Serves 6

Prawns and Scallops in Garlic

25 g (1 oz) butter
2 tablespoons oil
2 cloves garlic,
  crushed
250 g (8 oz) peeled
  prawns
8 shelled scallops,
  halved
2 tablespoons
  chopped parsley
juice of ½ lemon

Heat the butter and oil in a frying pan, add the garlic and fry for 2 minutes. Add the prawns and scallops and cook quickly for 2 minutes, or until the scallops are tender; take care not to overcook or they will become tough.

Stir in the parsley and lemon juice and serve immediately, with crusty bread.
Serves 4 to 6

Smoked Haddock Roulade

50 g (2 oz) plain
  flour
4 large eggs,
  separated
2 tablespoons water
125 g (4 oz)
  Cheddar cheese,
  grated
4 tablespoons grated
  Parmesan cheese
salt and pepper
FILLING:
25 g (1 oz) butter
25 g (1 oz) plain
  flour
200 ml (⅓ pint)
  milk
250 g (8 oz) smoked
  haddock fillets,
  cooked, skinned
  and flaked
1 hard-boiled egg,
  chopped
1 tablespoon chopped
  parsley
TO GARNISH:
herb sprigs

Sift the flour into a bowl and beat in the egg yolks and water until smooth. Stir in the Cheddar cheese, half the Parmesan cheese and salt and pepper to taste. Whisk the egg whites until stiff and carefully fold into the mixture.

Spread evenly into a lined and greased 30 × 20 cm (12 × 8 inch) Swiss roll tin and bake in a preheated moderately hot oven, 200°C (400°F), Gas Mark 6, for 12 to 15 minutes, until well risen and golden brown.

Meanwhile, melt the butter in a pan, add the flour and cook for 1 minute, stirring. Gradually stir in the milk and cook, stirring, for 1 minute. Season with salt and pepper to taste. Fold in the haddock, chopped egg and parsley.

Sprinkle the remaining Parmesan over a large piece of greaseproof paper. Turn the roulade onto this, removing the lining paper. Spread the filling over the surface and carefully roll up like a Swiss roll.

Serve immediately, while still hot, garnished with herbs.
Serves 6

Smoked Haddock Pancakes

500 g (1 lb) smoked
  haddock fillets
50 g (2 oz) butter
1 small onion, finely
  chopped
40 g (1½ oz) plain
  flour
300 ml (½ pint)
  milk
6 tablespoons double
  cream
1 tablespoon lemon
  juice
1 tablespoon chopped
  chives
1 tablespoon chopped
  parsley
125 g (4 oz)
  Cheddar cheese,
  grated
salt and pepper
2 tablespoons grated
  Parmesan cheese
PANCAKES:
125 g (4 oz) plain
  flour
pinch of salt
1 egg
scant 300 ml
  (½ pint) milk
2 tablespoons cold
  water
oil for shallow-frying
TO GARNISH:
lemon wedges
rosemary sprigs
  (optional)

First, make the pancakes. Sift the
flour and salt into a bowl, make a
well in the centre and add the egg
and half the milk. Mix until smooth.
Gradually add the remaining milk
and the water and beat until smooth.

Heat a little oil in a 15 to 18 cm (6
to 7 inch) frying pan. Pour in about
2 tablespoons batter and quickly tilt
the pan to coat the bottom evenly.
Cook until the underside is brown,
then turn the pancake over and
cook the other side. Repeat with
the remaining batter, to make
12 pancakes. Stack them on a plate,
with a sheet of greaseproof paper
between each, as they are cooked.

Place the haddock in a pan and add
just enough water to cover. Bring to
the boil, cover and poach gently for
10 minutes. Drain, then remove the
skin and any bones. Flake the fish.

Melt the butter in a pan, add the
onion and cook for 5 minutes,
without browning. Stir in the flour
and cook for 1 minute. Gradually
add the milk, stirring constantly,
bring to the boil and cook for
2 minutes. Stir in the cream, lemon
juice, herbs, Cheddar cheese, and
pepper to taste and stir until the
cheese has melted. Fold in the flaked
fish and season with salt to taste.

Divide the haddock mixture
between the pancakes and roll up.
Arrange in an ovenproof dish and
sprinkle with the Parmesan cheese.
Cover with a lid or foil and bake in
a preheated moderate oven, 180°C
(350°F), Gas Mark 4, for 20 to
25 minutes, until hot.

Uncover and return to the oven
for 5 minutes, until lightly browned.
Serve immediately, garnished with
lemon wedges and rosemary if using.
Serves 6

Marinated Kipper Fillets

500 g (1 lb) frozen
kipper fillets,
thawed
6 tablespoons olive oil
3 tablespoons lemon
juice
1 tablespoon chopped
parsley
1 tablespoon chopped
chives
pepper
TO GARNISH:
onion rings
lemon slices
parsley sprigs

Remove the skin and any bones from the kippers. Cut the fillets into thin slivers and put into a bowl.

Mix together the oil, lemon juice, herbs, and pepper to taste. Pour over the kippers and toss well to ensure that the fish is well coated. Cover and chill for 2 to 3 hours.

Transfer to a serving dish and garnish with onion rings, lemon slices and parsley sprigs. Serve with brown bread and butter.
Serves 6

PÂTÉS, TERRINES & MOUSSES

Smoked Salmon Pâté

250 g (8 oz) smoked
 salmon trimmings
50 g (2 oz) unsalted
 butter, softened
6 tablespoons lemon
 juice
salt
cayenne pepper
1 drop Tabasco sauce
1 tablespoon chopped
 chives
1 tablespoon chopped
 parsley
lemon slices to
 garnish

Remove any bones and skin from the salmon and mince or chop finely.

Cream the butter and 2 tablespoons of the lemon juice together, then beat in the salmon, and season with salt and cayenne pepper to taste. Add the Tabasco and remaining lemon juice and mix until the pâté is thick and creamy. Stir in the chives and parsley. Cover and chill until required.

Spoon the pâté into 4 individual dishes and garnish with lemon slices. Serve with hot buttered toast.

Serves 4

Smoked Mackerel Pâté

250 g (8 oz) smoked
  mackerel fillets
25 g (1 oz) unsalted
  butter
1 small onion, finely
  chopped
2 tablespoons flour
150 ml (¼ pint)
  milk
2 teaspoons lemon
  juice
1 tablespoon dry
  white wine
salt and pepper
150 ml (¼ pint)
  double cream,
  lightly whipped
TO GARNISH:
few lettuce leaves
cucumber twists

Remove the skin and bones from the
mackerel and flake the fish. Heat the
butter in a pan, add the onion and
cook for 5 to 7 minutes, without
browning.

Stir in the flour and cook for
2 minutes. Gradually stir in the milk
and cook, stirring, for 1 minute.
Transfer to a bowl.

Stir in the lemon juice and wine
and season liberally with salt and
pepper. Add the fish to the sauce and
beat until smooth. Fold in the cream.
Cover and chill until required.

Spoon the mixture into
4 individual dishes lined with lettuce
leaves. Decorate with cucumber
twists and serve with hot buttered
toast.

Serves 4

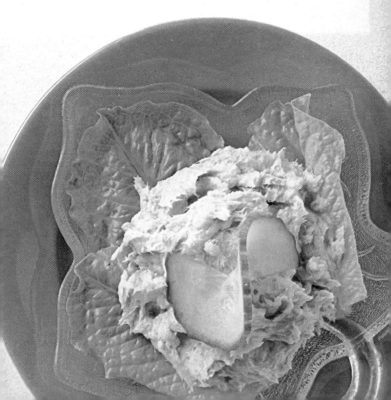

Ardennes Pâté

250 g (8 oz) pork
  fillet, diced
250 g (8 oz) belly
  pork, diced
250 g (8 oz) minced
  veal
350 g (12 oz) chicken
  livers, chopped
4 tablespoons brandy
2 teaspoons chopped
  thyme
1 tablespoon green
  peppercorns
  (optional)
salt and pepper
4-6 rashers streaky
  bacon, derinded
TO GARNISH:
thyme sprigs
lemon slices

Combine the pork, veal and chicken livers in a bowl. Stir in the brandy, thyme, peppercorns if using, and salt and pepper to taste. Cover and chill for 2 hours.

Spoon the mixture into a lightly greased 1 kg (2 lb) loaf tin. Stretch the bacon and use to cover the pâté. Cover with foil and place in a roasting pan. Pour in enough boiling water to come halfway up the sides of the pan. Cook in a preheated moderate oven, 180°C (350°F), Gas Mark 4, for 1½ hours.

Leave the pâté to cool in the tin; turn out when cold. Serve garnished with thyme and lemon slices, and accompanied by toast.
Serves 8

Sherried Chicken Liver Pâté

50 g (2 oz) butter
125 g (4 oz) back
  bacon, derinded
  and chopped
2 cloves garlic, crushed
1 small onion,
  chopped
500 g (1 lb) chicken
  livers, chopped
salt and pepper
2 thyme sprigs
2 parsley sprigs
125 g (4 oz) button
  mushrooms,
  chopped
4 tablespoons dry
  sherry
4 tablespoons double
  cream
1 teaspoon lemon
  juice
watercress sprigs to
  garnish

Melt the butter in a pan, add the bacon, garlic and onion and cook gently for 3 minutes. Stir in the chicken livers and cook for 5 minutes. Season liberally with salt and pepper. Stir in the herbs and mushrooms. Add the sherry and cook until the liquid has evaporated. Cool, then work in an electric blender until smooth. Stir in the cream and lemon juice.

Spoon into a greased ovenproof dish. Cover with a lid and stand in a roasting pan, containing water to a depth of 2.5 cm (1 inch). Bake in a preheated cool oven, 150°C (300°F), Gas Mark 2, for 2 to 2½ hours, until cooked through. Allow to cool. Cover and chill until required.

Divide the pâté between individual plates and garnish with watercress. Serve with hot buttered toast.
Serves 6

Terrine de Canard

*1 × 1.5 kg (3 lb)
    oven-ready duck,
    skin and bones
    removed
500 g (1 lb) minced
    pork
350 g (12 oz)
    minced veal
1 clove garlic, crushed
1 tablespoon Worcester-
    shire sauce
juice of 1 orange
2 teaspoons dried
    mixed herbs
150 ml (¼ pint) dry
    red wine
salt and pepper
10 rashers streaky
    bacon, derinded
1 tablespoon brandy*
TO GARNISH:
*orange twists
watercress sprigs*

Dice the duck meat and mix with the
pork and veal. Add the garlic,
Worcestershire sauce, orange juice,
herbs, wine, and salt and pepper to
taste. Cover and chill overnight.

Using a sharp knife, stretch the
bacon rashers and use to line the base
and sides of a 1 kg (2 lb) terrine or
loaf tin. Press the meat mixture into
the tin, sprinkle with the brandy and
cover with foil.

Place in a roasting pan and pour in
enough boiling water to come halfway up the sides of the pan. Cook in
a preheated moderate oven, 180°C
(350°F), Gas Mark 4, for 1½ to
1¾ hours.

Leave until cold then turn out onto
a serving dish. Serve garnished with
orange twists and watercress.
Serves 8

Terrine of Chicken

40 g (1½ oz) butter
50 g (2 oz) button
  mushrooms,
  chopped
1 clove garlic,
  roughly chopped
500 g (1 lb) chicken
  livers, chopped
3 tablespoons dry red
  wine
1 teaspoon chopped
  thyme
salt
1 tablespoon brandy
1 tablespoon single
  cream
250 g (8 oz) boned
  chicken, thinly
  sliced
2 tablespoons green
  peppercorns
lettuce leaves to
  garnish

Melt half the butter in a pan, add the mushrooms and cook for 2 minutes. Remove with a slotted spoon and set aside. Add the remaining butter and garlic to the pan; cook for 1 minute. Add the chicken livers and cook for 5 minutes. Add the wine, thyme, and salt to taste. Cook for 15 minutes.

Work the mixture in an electric blender until smooth, then stir in the mushrooms, brandy and cream.

Spoon a thin layer of liver mixture into a lightly greased 500 g (1 lb) terrine. Cover with a layer of chicken, then sprinkle with a few peppercorns. Repeat layers until all the ingredients are used, finishing with liver mixture. Cover with a lid or foil.

Stand the dish in a roasting pan containing enough boiling water to come halfway up the sides of the dish. Cook in a preheated moderate oven, 180°C (350°F), Gas Mark 4, for 1 to 1¼ hours. Cool, then chill until required. Garnish with lettuce and serve with toast.

Serves 6 to 8

Asparagus and Crab Mousse

1 × 340 g (12 oz)
  can asparagus
1 × 177 g (6 oz)
  can crabmeat
150 ml (¼ pint)
  chicken or fish
  stock
  (approximately)
25 g (1 oz) butter
25 g (1 oz) plain
  flour
15 g (½ oz) gelatine
3 tablespoons dry
  white wine
300 ml (½ pint)
  mayonnaise
150 ml (¼ pint)
  double cream,
  lightly whipped
lemon slices or whole
  prawns to garnish

Drain and reserve the liquid from the asparagus and crabmeat, adding sufficient stock to make 300 ml (½ pint).

Melt the butter in a pan, stir in the flour and cook for 1 minute. Stir in the stock, bring to the boil and simmer, stirring, for 2 minutes. Roughly chop the asparagus and flake the crabmeat. Fold into the sauce.

Dissolve the gelatine in the wine over low heat, then stir into the asparagus mixture. Fold in the mayonnaise and cream. Spoon the mixture into an 18 cm (7 inch) round tin or mould and chill until set.

Turn out onto a serving dish and garnish with lemon slices or whole prawns.
Serves 6 to 8

Cheddar and Prawn Mousse

2 eggs, separated
125 g (4 oz)
  matured Cheddar
  cheese, finely
  grated
1 tablespoon grated
  Parmesan cheese
2 teaspoons English
  mustard
cayenne pepper
grated nutmeg
salt
284 ml (10 fl oz)
  double cream
50 g (2 oz) peeled
  prawns, chopped
TO GARNISH:
whole prawns
  (optional)
lemon slices

Beat the egg yolks until pale in colour. Mix in the cheeses, mustard and cayenne, nutmeg and salt to taste.

Whip the cream until it just holds its shape. Fold into the cheese mixture with the prawns. Whisk the egg whites until stiff, then fold into the mixture.

Spoon into 4 ramekin dishes and chill until required.

Serve garnished with prawns if using, and lemon slices.
Serves 4

Smoked Trout Mousse

3 smoked trout
300 ml (½ pint) dry
white wine
2 teaspoons finely
chopped onion
½ clove garlic, crushed
1 parsley sprig
2 tarragon sprigs
1 thyme sprig
2 bay leaves
salt and pepper
284 ml (10 fl oz)
soured cream
TO GARNISH:
lemon or lime slices
parsley sprigs

Place the trout in a pan with the wine,
onion, garlic, herbs, and salt and
pepper to taste. Cover and cook
gently for 10 minutes. Lift the fish
from the pan, reserving the cooking
liquor. Discard the skin and bones;
place the fish in an electric blender.

Boil the cooking liquor until
reduced by one third, then strain into
the blender and work to a purée.
Turn into a bowl and fold in the
cream. Cover and chill until required.

Spoon into individual dishes and
garnish with lemon or lime slices and
parsley.
Serves 4 to 6

PASTA & RICE DISHES

Fettuccine with Cream and Mushroom Sauce

500 g (1 lb) plain or
  spinach noodles
  (fettuccine)
salt and pepper
50 g (2 oz) butter
1 clove garlic, crushed
175 g (6 oz) button
  mushrooms, sliced
120 ml (4 fl oz)
  double cream
2 egg yolks
grated Parmesan
  cheese to serve

Cook the noodles in boiling salted water for 10 to 12 minutes, until just tender.

Meanwhile, melt the butter in a pan, add the garlic and cook for 1 minute, without browning. Add the mushrooms and fry for 2 minutes. Add the cream and simmer for 10 minutes. Season with salt and pepper to taste. Remove from the heat, leave for 2 minutes, then stir in the egg yolks.

Drain the pasta and add to the sauce; toss well.

Serve immediately, with Parmesan cheese.

Serves 6

Spaghetti with Mussels

1 kg (2 lb) mussels
   in shells, scrubbed
   clean
2 tablespoons olive
   oil
1 small onion, finely
   chopped
2-3 cloves garlic,
   crushed
1 × 397 g (14 oz)
   can tomatoes
3 tablespoons tomato
   purée
2 tablespoons dry
   white wine
2 tablespoons
   chopped parsley
1 bouquet garni
salt and pepper
350 g (12 oz)
   spaghetti
Parmesan cheese to
   serve

Put the mussels in a pan of boiling water and cook for about 5 minutes, until the shells have opened; discard any that do not. Shell the mussels and set aside.

Heat the oil in a pan, add the onion and garlic and cook gently for 5 to 7 minutes. Stir in the tomatoes with their juice, tomato purée and wine and bring to the boil. Stir in the parsley, bouquet garni, and salt and pepper to taste. Cook, uncovered, for 25 to 30 minutes, until thickened.

Meanwhile, cook the spaghetti in boiling salted water for 10 to 12 minutes until just tender; drain thoroughly.

Discard the bouquet garni and add the mussels to the sauce; heat through gently. Add the sauce to the spaghetti and toss well. Serve immediately, with Parmesan.

Serves 4 to 6

Ravioli

DOUGH:
250 g (8 oz) strong
   plain flour
good pinch of salt
50 g (2 oz) butter,
   softened
little boiling water to
   mix

FILLING:
125 g (4 oz) grated
   Parmesan cheese
175 g (6 oz)
   Gruyère cheese,
   grated
3 eggs, beaten
1 teaspoon grated
   nutmeg
1 teaspoon each
   chopped basil and
   marjoram
salt and pepper
little milk to mix (if
   necessary)

TO SERVE:
grated Parmesan
   cheese
chopped herbs

Sift the flour and salt into a bowl.
Rub in the butter until the mixture
resembles breadcrumbs. Add
sufficient boiling water to give a
pliable but firm dough. Turn onto a
floured surface and knead well.
Divide the dough in half, wrap in
cling film and set aside.

Mix together the cheeses, eggs,
nutmeg, herbs, and salt and pepper
to taste to give a firm mixture,
adding a little milk if it is too stiff.

Roll out both pieces of dough on a
floured surface until paper thin.

Place teaspoonfuls of the cheese
and herb mixture on one piece of
dough at 3.5 cm (1½ inch) intervals.
Cover with the second sheet of pasta,
without stretching it. Lightly press
down around the mounds of filling.
Using a pastry wheel, separate each
ravioli, making sure the edges are
sealed. Leave to dry for 2 to 3 hours.

Cook in boiling salted water for
4 to 5 minutes. Drain and serve,
with plenty of Parmesan and herbs.
Serves 6

Cannelloni

8 sheets of lasagne

FILLING:

2 tablespoons oil
1 onion, chopped
2 cloves garlic, crushed
250 g (8 oz) ground
    beef
4 tomatoes, skinned,
    seeded and chopped
1 tablespoon tomato
    purée
2 tablespoons red wine
salt and pepper
2 tablespoons fresh
    white breadcrumbs
25 g (1 oz) grated
    Parmesan cheese
1 teaspoon chopped
    marjoram
1 egg, beaten

CHEESE SAUCE:

40 g (1½ oz) butter
40 g (1½ oz) flour
300 ml (½ pint) milk
150 ml (¼ pint)
    double cream
grated nutmeg
125 g (4 oz) Cheddar
    cheese, grated

To make the filling, heat the oil in a pan, add the onion and garlic and cook until golden. Add the beef and cook, stirring, until browned. Stir in the tomatoes, tomato purée, wine, and salt and pepper to taste. Cover and simmer for 30 minutes. Cool, then stir in the breadcrumbs, Parmesan, marjoram and egg.

Cook the lasagne in boiling salted water for 10 to 12 minutes, until just tender. Drain thoroughly. Lay the sheets of pasta on oiled greaseproof paper and divide the filling between them. Roll up and place side by side in an ovenproof dish.

For the cheese sauce, melt the butter in a pan, stir in the flour and cook for 1 minute. Gradually stir in the milk. Add the cream and salt, pepper and nutmeg to taste. Add the cheese and stir until melted.

Spoon the sauce over the cannelloni. Cover and cook in a preheated moderately hot oven, 200°C (400°F), Gas Mark 6, for 25 minutes. Remove lid and cook for a further 5 minutes or until golden brown. Serve hot.
Serves 6 to 8

Tortellini Bolognese

25 g (1 oz) butter
125 g (4 oz) lean pork, chopped
75 g (3 oz) lean veal, chopped
1 small chicken breast, chopped
50 g (2 oz) cooked ham, chopped
25 g (1 oz) Mortadella, chopped
salt and pepper
75 g (3 oz) grated Parmesan cheese
2 eggs
½ teaspoon grated nutmeg
500 g (1 lb) plain flour
pinch of salt
3 eggs
cold water to mix
melted butter and grated Parmesan cheese to serve

Melt the butter in a pan, add the pork, veal and chicken and brown lightly. Add the ham, Mortadella, and salt and pepper to taste. Cover and cook for 15 minutes. Cool slightly, then mince the meat. Mix in the Parmesan, eggs and nutmeg.

Sift the flour and salt onto a board, make a hollow in the centre and add the eggs. Work to a stiff dough, adding a little water if necessary. With floured hands, knead until smooth. Roll out on a floured surface until paper thin. Using a 4 cm (1½ inch) fluted cutter, cut into rounds.

Spoon a little filling onto each round, dampen the edges, then fold to form semi-circles. Curl them, bringing the two points together. Place on a floured tray, cover with a cloth and leave to dry for 12 hours.

Cook in boiling salted water for 5 to 7 minutes; drain. Toss in melted butter and sprinkle liberally with grated Parmesan cheese to serve.
Serves 6 to 8

Seafood Risotto

50 g (2 oz) butter
1 large onion, finely
    chopped
2 cloves garlic,
    crushed
350 g (12 oz)
    Italian rice
300 ml (½ pint) dry
    white wine
1 bouquet garni
salt and pepper
1 litre (1¾ pints)
    chicken stock
    (approximately)
6 shelled scallops,
    chopped
12 mussels in shells,
    scrubbed clean
12 cooked unshelled
    prawns
4 tablespoons grated
    Parmesan cheese
2 tablespoons
    chopped parsley

Melt the butter in a pan, add the
onion and garlic and cook until
lightly browned. Stir in the rice and
wine. Add the bouquet garni and salt
and pepper to taste. Pour in two
thirds of the stock, bring to the boil
and cook rapidly for 10 minutes.

Meanwhile, cook the scallops and
mussels in boiling salted water for
about 5 minutes until the mussel
shells have opened; discard any that
do not. Drain thoroughly.

Add the scallops and mussels to
the rice with the prawns. Add more
stock if necessary: do not allow the
risotto to become dry. Heat through
gently for 3 to 5 minutes, until the
rice is cooked and the liquid is
absorbed. Discard the bouquet garni.

Stir in the Parmesan and parsley
and serve hot.
Serves 6 to 8

Risotto with Mushrooms

8 dried mushrooms
  (optional)
50 g (2 oz) butter
1 onion, finely
  chopped
1 clove garlic, thinly
  sliced
350 g (12 oz)
  Italian rice
250 ml (8 fl oz) dry
  white wine
salt and pepper
300 ml (½ pint)
  chicken stock
  (approximately)
1 bouquet garni
125 g (4 oz) button
  mushrooms, sliced
pinch of powdered
  saffron
50 g (2 oz) grated
  Parmesan cheese

Soak the dried mushrooms in warm water for 15 minutes, if using. Squeeze dry, remove the hard stalks and chop the mushroom caps. Keep on one side.

Melt the butter in a pan, add the onion and garlic and cook for 10 minutes or until lightly browned. Stir in the rice and wine. Bring to the boil and boil rapidly until the wine is reduced by half. Add two thirds of the stock, bouquet garni and salt and pepper to taste. Simmer, uncovered, for 12 to 15 minutes, until the rice is just tender; add stock if necessary to prevent the risotto becoming dry.

Add all the mushrooms and the saffron; cook for 3 minutes. Remove the bouquet garni and check the seasoning. Sprinkle with the Parmesan and serve immediately.
Serves 6

Chicken Liver Pilaff

125 g (4 oz) streaky
  bacon
25 g (1 oz) butter
2 cloves garlic, thinly
  sliced
250 g (8 oz) chicken
  livers, chopped
50 g (2 oz) button
  mushrooms, sliced
250 ml (8 fl oz) dry
  white wine
1 bouquet garni
175 g (6 oz) long-
  grain rice
salt and pepper
300 ml (½ pint)
  chicken stock
3 tablespoons single
  cream
2 tablespoons
  chopped parsley

Remove the rinds from the bacon and cut into small pieces.

Melt the butter in a pan, add the bacon and sauté gently for 2 minutes. Add the garlic and chicken livers and cook for 5 minutes, stirring occasionally. Add the mushrooms, wine, bouquet garni, rice and salt and pepper to taste. Stir in the stock, bring to the boil, cover and simmer for 12 minutes.

Remove the lid, increase the heat, and stir until the rice is just tender and all the liquid has been absorbed. Discard the bouquet garni.

Just before serving, stir in the cream and parsley. Serve immediately, garnished with lemon twists.
Serves 4 to 6

INDEX